START TRADING USING TECHNICAL ANALYSIS

WAKING UP EVERY DAY KNOWING THERE WILL BE AN EXTRA $100 IN YOUR BANK ACCOUNT

LINA SOROS

CONTENTS

A Special Gift To Our Readers   v
Introduction   vii

1. INTRODUCTION TO TRADING   1
   Scalp Trading   2
   Range Trading   12
   High-Frequency Teading (HFT)   19

2. TECHNICAL ANALYSIS   27
   Dow Theory: The Six Tenets   31

3. CHART READING AND ITS RELEVANCE IN TRADING   43
   The 3 Universal Principles of Trading   43
   Core Elements of Trading   45
   Understanding the Basics of Trading Charts   48

4. TREND REVERSALS: A TREND BECOMING AN OPPOSITE TREND   53
   Sharp Trend Reversal   64
   Major Trend Reversal   74
   How To Trade Reversal   87
   Signs Of Strength In Reversal   88

5. STOP-LOSS ORDERS   94
   Understanding the Basics   94
   Stop-Loss Placement Methods   95
   Theoretical analysis of the Bear Markets   95

6. THE BEST TRADES: PUTTING IT ALL TOGETHER   101
   Examples Of Best Trades   108
   Top 10 Rules For Successful Trading   112
   How Much Do You Buy or Sell?   113

Conclusion   115

© Copyright 2021 - All rights reserved.

The content contained within this book may not be reproduced, duplicated or transmitted without direct written permission from the author or the publisher.

Under no circumstances will any blame or legal responsibility be held against the publisher, or author, for any damages, reparation, or monetary loss due to the information contained within this book. Either directly or indirectly. You are responsible for your own choices, actions, and results.

Legal Notice:

This book is copyright protected. This book is only for personal use. You cannot amend, distribute, sell, use, quote or paraphrase any part, or the content within this book, without the consent of the author or publisher.

Disclaimer Notice:

Please note the information contained within this document is for educational and entertainment purposes only. All effort has been executed to present accurate, up to date, and reliable, complete information. No warranties of any kind are declared or implied. Readers acknowledge that the author is not engaging in the rendering of legal, financial, medical or professional advice. The content within this book has been derived from various sources. Please consult a licensed professional before attempting any techniques outlined in this book.

By reading this document, the reader agrees that under no circumstances is the author responsible for any losses, direct or indirect, which are incurred as a result of the use of the information contained within this document, including, but not limited to, — errors, omissions, or inaccuracies.

A SPECIAL GIFT TO OUR READERS

The file can't be downloaded from the following link
https://linasorospublishing.activehosted.com/f/1

INTRODUCTION

Treat trading as a business and have a proper plan to succeed. Enter the trade with a belief in analysis but forecasting. And as you become a successful trader, become a change agent in society by giving back.

I found interest in trading in 2002 and began professionally in 2004. Before I started trading, I had already opened an account with Zecco, a discount brokerage firm in existence for years now. Zecco recently merged with Tradeking, which also didn't sustain sole proprietorship for long as Ally Invest acquired it in 2016. Before my first trial in trading, I researched "best" trading practices and strategies; I made sure to have a sound knowledge of these strategies and techniques before making investments. Knowing full well that there could be downsides, I started off trading with $2000 and set that as a limit. From my research, I discovered that options and equities were suitable forms of trading, so I started with these two forms, and after a while, I moved to the pink sheets.

You're wondering what "pink sheets" means. Well, here you go; Pink sheets are referred to as an OTC market; they are over-the-counter markets that connect small-scale traders electronically. There's nothing like a trading market in pink sheets as all activities, including quotations, are all done electronically. In the absence of a trading market or stock exchange like other trading platforms like the New York Stock Exchange (NYSE), companies listed as pink sheets do not have the same policies as companies listed on NSE. Therefore, they do not have to follow the rules like the national stock exchange companies. Pink sheets companies are allowed to sell stocks for as low as $5 a share. These kinds of stocks are regarded as low-prices penny stocks. I guess you can see why I moved to the pink sheets, funds management! However, I did not hang around the pink sheets for long. I paid more attention to several company news and technical analysis, which would be further discussed as you read this book. I churned out $48,000 from $2,000 in under a year and six months. Good profit, yeah? Definitely, but it was short-lived as financial crises occurred, and I lost about $24,000. This loss pushed me to pull out the cash I had left and take a break from trading until I could decide a better plan to tackle financial crises in trading.

The financial crisis had a massive effect on my turnout, but I wasn't discouraged because I had this strong feeling that there was more money to be made. All I needed was a better plan. I realized then that the pink sheets although works but wasn't consistent because it's thinly patronized. I couldn't wrap my head around the pink sheets penny stock investment and build a much better plan because I did not have enough data. Additionally, studying penny stock and paying attention to every update in the pink sheets companies was time-consuming. I wasn't able to focus on my graduate studies and carry out other personal activities at the time. I then decided so I just had to take a few steps backs and properly define what my relationship with the trading/stock market will turn out to be in the long run. During this period, I came up with some personal approaches for staying out of trouble in the financial markets and maximizing profits. In addition, I offer good insights into:

• The psychology behind proper risk control, as well as the important and crucial aspects of setting stop-loss, exist

• The value of managing trade size and consistent record-keeping

• Chart examples of early Warning Signs that function as Exit Indicators for a trade.

After a couple of research, I had decided that my time horizon wasn't seconds, minutes, nor hours. I should instead work with days and weeks. Having agreed on the timeframe windows, I readjusted my trading strategy, focusing on long and midterm trends. Following my new trading strategy, I followed the financials, recent, events, stocks for several weeks. With the data collected, I forecasted where the bottom would be for different financial stocks, and guess what? My predictions were correct! This strategy spiked my turnout rates as in 2009. I realized profits of over 350% within weeks for every stock market investment I made. At this time, I saw my profit rate as outstanding, and I took my time to analyze the strategy I was using turns out to be similar to the "value investing" approach. Read on and learn more about this strategy.

Fundamental analysis was one of the primary tools I was using for trading during this period. I used it to determine the intrinsic value for stock markets. I used it as a marker when carrying out trading activities in the bear market, buying and selling during financial downsides. When I thought my strategy was gold, the bulk market came, and my strategy became ineffective. The bulk markets were outrageous as every stock kept hitting new 52 week highs. Value and long-term bottom stocks were no longer available in the market. I had a re-think and decided to realign my strategy. Since the problem here was due to sudden spikes in market values, I started focusing more on momentum indicators, but I did something unique this time. Instead of restricting myself to buying individual company stocks, I decided to be more diverse by patronizing more liquid ETFs. Picking up about 20 ETFs, I started my trading adventure using this strategy without wasting any more time on screenings. Once bitten twice shy, I reserved 10% of my total capital for other investments if financial crises occur in my new strategies. I was switching my strategies with the former ones I had used because ETFs weren't consistent over the years relative to other strategies I had devised. However, during the periods when I switched, I did not discard all my ETFs. Instead, I held a few inverse ETFs after monitoring their progress over the years and seeing potentials them. As a result, I've found success in trading, and I'm becoming more diverse. I figured I couldn't afford to spend as much time studying charts, so I decided to buy the idea of building an automated trader that will carry out trades for me with the strategies I instruct it to use. Computerized traders are available with several brokerage firms.

However, traders have to meet specific requirements to gain access to these automated traders. One of the strategies I instructed my automated trader to use, which would be discussed later in this book, is technical analysis. Even after ordering the automated trader to use technical analysis strategies while making trades, I still had to monitor its actions from time to time. I've learned a lot as a trader, and one of the essential things I've learned is that you will always find a pattern in any phenomenon in nature. However, the patterns devised aren't permanent. It's rare for a trader to stick to a particular way for an extended period and succeed in all trades. There will always be downsides. This is a crucial trading lesson you should hold on to.

In this book, we will walk through insider secrets for making cash from your home or anywhere across the globe, the essential basics that all beginners should know about technical analysis. Likely, you'll also need indicators in carrying out trading activities. You will be able to systematically discuss market indicators and use them effectively when you're done reading this book. Most professional traders use RSI indicators, while others use the 50-200 days monitoring technique. The indicator type that will work best for you might be different from the two types mentioned. You'll find your type of indicator as you read on. Although there are many odds to consider when working with indicators, this book simplifies everything for the reader. So basically, you'll find something that works for you without having to put in much effort. Throughout my journey in the stock and options markets, I have been a hedge fund manager, investment advisor, advisor to the floor and desk traders and portfolio managers, institutional stockbroker, options trader, desk and large-block trader, lecturer, and speaker on aspects of technical analysis to professional and academic groups. I'm also an owner of an institutional brokerage firm.

Helping you become an expert in spotting market trends and key indicators matters deeply because what you're about to learn helped me achieve excellent stock market results, financial freedom, and become a successful trader.

Are you ready to get equipped with instrumental knowledge on using simple technical analysis to conquer the stock market and reel in gains that dreams are made of? Ride on with me.

1

INTRODUCTION TO TRADING

There was once when people did not know much about trading, which affected the growth of trading in the economy as people were only actively involved in stock market trading activities, brokerages, and trading firms. However, with the advancement of technology and trading firms, trading has been expanded. As a result, an average investor can control several types of trade types at ease as long as the basics are understood.

Of all methods of trading, Day trading is the most popular among investors. It turns out to be the most popular because it's a lucrative career if handled right away. However, day trading could be a challenge, especially for novices who aren't well schooled on day trading strategies which will later be discussed in this chapter. Newbies encounter problems with day trading. Professionals in the career also hit rough patches and suffer losses. Our central idea in this chapter will be "day trading a major form of trading," and this is because its concept adequately explains what trading is all about.

. . .

To begin with, let's talk about what exactly day trading is all about and how it operates.

Investors who engage in day trading are active traders who monitor market prices every day to profit off fluctuations of different assets. Day traders need to know several day trading techniques to capitalize on all market fluctuations. Day trading is closely related to technical analysis, meaning it also requires a certain level of self-discipline and commitment.

As a day trader, your daily hustle will involve buying and selling securities. You can carry day trader in any marketplace, stock markets, forex, and lots more. Day traders often have solid educational backgrounds and are also well-funded. They invest with high amounts on minor price fluctuations that occur within minutes or a few hours. Day traders are always conversant of events that cause market price fluctuations. If you stay with a day trader, you'll notice that they hardly miss market price news or announcement. Asides from some professional strategies used by day traders, staying attuned to market price news is also a strategy used by day traders.

Standard strategies used by day traders include:

Scalp Trading

Scalping is a trading style that involves making a profit off small price fluctuations and through market re-sale. Day traders often encounter small price fluctuations; this makes Scalping one of the best strategies for them. Asa day trader using the scalping strategy, you're also expected to have a good escape strategy. This is because a single loss in day trading could ruin all a day trader's lifetime earnings. Thus, knowing the right moves and having the right tools such as an access broker, live feed, and a stable market are necessary for you to successfully use this strategy. Professional stock scalpers have a higher winning rate than losing, although the ratio of their profits to losses isn't always wide. Scalpers make hundreds of trades in under 24 hours. I bet you're wondering how Scalping works. Well, here you go;

Scalping is largely based on calculated predictions on stock movements. It involves predicting that stocks will pull through the first stage of price movement. However, stocks act funny after the first stage of the movement, making it difficult for scalpers to predict their next move after the initial step. After the first stage, a stock could either cease to advance by crashing or gain higher grounds and continue advancing.

Scalping works with the principle of increasing your winning rates by sacrificing your win size. This is the direct opposite of the "let your returns run your trade" mindset, which focuses on manipulating trading strategies to yield positive outcomes and increase the size of wins.

It's common among long-term traders to achieve positive winning statistics by succeeding in only half of their total trading activities, or even less because they are after the size of wins and not the rate of wins. On the other hand, a successful scalper will always have a higher ratio of wins to losses at the end of a trading year, keeping the size of their profits almost equal to the size of their failures or slightly more prominent. Check out what a scalp trading technique looks like below:

Let's get familiar with the logic behind Scalping by checking out these few tenets:

➔ Lessened risk exposure

Fast buying and selling of market prices using fluctuations in seconds/minutes reduce your chances of running at a loss.

➔ Smaller moves with more minor technicalities are obtained

Continuous fluctuations of supply and demand are essential for massive changes in market prices. Take, for instance. It's easier for a stock to make a $0.02 move than for making a $2 move.

➔ Smaller moves occur more frequently than massive ones

Scalpers enjoy lots of small price fluctuations, even during periods where markets are quiet. This leaves scalpers with several earning opportunities.

SCALPING COULD BE ADOPTED as a primary or supplementary trading system. But before we just in that discussion, let's walk through a comparison between spreads in Scalping and spreads in general trading strategies.

When scalpers trade, their mindset is making a profit off any minor fluctuations in market prices bid-ask spread. The bid-ask price is the difference between a broker's proposed price for buying security, and the broker's price will most likely sell the security to the scalper. So basically, the scalper is in search of a narrower spread.

However, in regular trading circumstances, trading is consistent to an extent as fluctuations occur most of the time, hence, an opportunity for steady profit acquisition. Trade consistency is due to the steadiness of the spread in the bid-ask relationship. This means there's a balance in the demand and supply of assets.

Moving on, let's now discuss Scalping as a primary/supplementary trading style.

AS A PRIMARY TRADING STYLE:

A typical scalper makes hundreds of trades daily. Using ticks or a few seconds charts, scalpers can come about setups that work very closely with real-time since the period is minute. Arrangements like Direct Access Trading and Level 2 quotes are essential for day trading using the scalping strategy.

Scalpers also embrace the direct-access broker system as rapid execution of trading activities is needed.

As a Supplementary Style:

Long-term traders use Scalping as a supplementary style of trading. The obvious way of using it is by activating it when market prices are locked and narrow assets. However, in a longer time frame when there is no trends insight, going for the short-term option will always surface, and this could lead to a long-term trader being a scalper.

Although this could make it seem like Scalping can not be used for long-term trades well, that's not the case. One can also use Scalping for long-term trades using the "umbrella" concept. The umbrella approach shows that traders can also maximize profit in long-term trades. Here's how it works:

- A trader sets up a position for the long-term trade

While the original trade format developed progresses, the trader creates new setups for short-term trades in the leading trade's direction, monitoring and carrying out trading activities using the scalping principle.

- Scalping works perfectly with a trading system

Scalping can be conveniently seen as an excellent system for risk management. Technically, any trading system could be converted into a scalp by considering profit close to the 1:1 reward ratio. This means that the profit size is equal to the half-size that the setup dictates. Take, for example, a trader entering a stable position for Scalping at $30 with an initial stop at $29.90. From the calculation, the risk here is $0.10, and this technically means that a 1:1 reward ratio will be attained at $30.10.

- SCALP TRADES can be executed either on long or short sides

This happens mostly during breakouts. Many local chart formations like triangles, cups, or even handles, could be utilized for scalp trades. On this feature, scalp trading is closely related to indicator trading, especially when a trader bases decisions on them.

Scalping only works for traders if done the right way following the right strategies. This leads us to the different scalping strategies:

- THE FIRST type of scalping strategy is "market-making"

In market-making, the scalper tries to bank entirely on the spread by posting a bid and offer for a market at the same time. The market-making strategy can prosper only on immobile market prices that trade large volumes without severe price fluctuation.

This scalping strategy could be challenging because a trader is expected to compete with market indicators for the assets on bids and offers. In addition to this, the profit is so little that any price fluctuation against the trader will demand a loss margin, exceeding their profit level expectations.

. . .

THE OTHER SCALPING strategies work on a more traditional approach compared to "market-marking." These strategies require a moving stock, where fluctuations happen rapidly. These strategies also demand a high level of commitment and a suitable method of chart reading.

The second scalping strategy is done by buying many shares disposed of again following a slight price fluctuation. A trader using this strategy will enter positions for many shares and patiently wait for a slight price fluctuation. Little price movements like this are usually measured in cents. Again, liquid stocks are needed for success using this strategy because liquid stocks make entry to and exit from shares quickly.

The last strategy we will be discussing is close to the traditional trading methods. It involves a trader inputting a specific amount of shares on any setup or signal originating from their system and closing the position immediately after the first exit signal is noticed. The first signal is near the 1:1 risk/reward ratio.

TALK About Tips for Scalp Traders?

With reduced entry barriers in the trading world, the number of investors trying their hands at day trading and other strategies for trading, Scalping inclusive, has spiked. Novices to the scalping trading strategy need to make sure the process is in accordance with their disposal. Scalping requires discipline, meaning a carefree trader will have difficulties succeeding with it.

Traders will also be expected to make swift decisions and use opportunities as soon as they show up. Therefore, they need to monitor the screen at all times. Impatient investors that are eager to make profits are perfect for Scalping.

That being said, Scalping might not be the best trading strategy for novices, and this is mainly because it requires speed, making crazy decisions within short periods, constantly monitoring price positions and turnovers. Asides from this tip, there are some other tips we would like to share with you:

- ORDER EXECUTION

Beginners must understand the art of effective order of execution adequately. A bad order is dangerous, a threat to your portfolio, and could wipe out the little profit you've earned. Since the level of profit per trading activity is limited, the order execution has to be perfect. As mentioned earlier in this book, the DAT- Direct Access Trading Tool is crucial in trading. Here is one of the instances where the tool is needed.

- COSTS and Frequencies

A rookie scalper has to make costs a top priority during trading. Scalping involves series of trades, all happening concurrently. Steady buying and selling are bound to be expensive when commissions are considered, which could affect the profit margin. This makes the tenet crucial for you to choose the correct broker. The broker will provide you with insights and provide the trader with very competitive commissions. Have it at the back of your mind that not all brokers allow Scalping.

. . .

- TRADING

Applying the trend and following the momentum appears easy for scalpers who enter and exit trading sessions briefly and repeat the same pattern continuously. However, as a rookie, you need to understand the concept behind "market pulse," once you understand the concept, you will be able to monitor trading trends and momentum and, in the end, achieve more profitable trades. Countertrend is another strategy you should be inclined with as a rookie scalper. However, don't always use the countertrend strategies in your rookie stage. Instead, stick to everyday trading ethics as a rookie.

- TECHNICAL ANALYSIS

Technical analysis is also a crucial strategy in the trading profession. Later on in this book, we will broadly discuss technical analysis, so just keep reading. Rookies should learn to equip themselves with the basics of technical analysis and, most importantly, its application. Technical analysis is relevant in today's market trends as HFT. High-frequency trading remains domineering. The technical indicator appropriate for Scalping that all rookies should be familiar with is called multiple chart scalping.

Technical analysis teaches you how to create and monitor charts without pressure. In addition, this strategy prepares you for actual trading activities.

. . .

- Discipline

In Scalping, it's best to conclude all trading activities for a day on that same day. Avoid procrastination, don't pile up trading activities. Scalping deals with expanding on small opportunities that could be found in the market; a scalper does not deviate from the basic tenet of monitoring specific positions for a short period.

Surprisingly, Scalping also has its wrong sides. So before we go through some of the cons of scalp trading, let's discuss why you should involve in scalp trading, what you stand to gain as a scalper.

WHAT DO I stand to gain from being a scalper?

One of the most significant advantages of being a good scalper is being very lucrative. Scalpers can easily leverage small price fluctuations that may not have any significant impact on the market trend. Just as we now know that scalpers don't play an important role when dealing with short-term trends, and it's for this reason that traders don't need to have vast knowledge about the stock market. Here are some other benefits of being a scalper:

- Huge profit margins could be realized if executed accurately
- Scalpers don't necessarily have to follow basic principles, and this makes the technique less risky
- Scalpers can function even when the market isn't stable. It's a non-directional trading strategy
- The scalping technique could easily be automated

Why you might have to reconsider using the scalping technique

All trading techniques have their disbenefits. Cons of the scalping technique include:

- Higher market prices when scalp trading technique is used
- Requires higher leverage when it comes to making a profit
- Scalping is time-consuming and requires an increased focus level

Range Trading

Forex traders mainly patronize range trading. It involves finding currencies that are oversold or overbought. The idea behind the range trading technique is buying stock during oversold periods and selling them during resistance/overbought periods.

A unique thing about range trading is that it could be implemented at any time, but it's most yielding when the market lacks direction, and as a trader, you can barely see a discernible long-term trend forthcoming. A trending market is the worst time to employ the range trading strategy, especially when the market isn't adequately accounted for. In 2017, currency markets suffered sideways. This made 2017 a great year for traders using the range trading strategy.

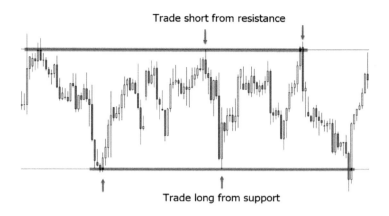

What is the type of range you'll most likely come across as a trader?

Do you want to become successful as a trader using the range trading technique? Then you'll need to have sound knowledge of the different types of ranges, their whole concepts, benefits, and disbenefits associated with using each type of range. Let's go through the four common types of ranges used by range traders.

- RECTANGULAR RANGE

A typical rectangular range will have sideways and horizontal price fluctuations between the oversold and overbought periods. This is rampant in most market trends but not as common as other ranges like channel or continuation ranges.

In a rectangular range chart, you'll notice the price fluctuation of currency pairs within the oversold and overbought periods; this tends to create a shape in the form of a rectangle—the rectangular sets clear parameters for sales opportunity identification.

Even without indicators, spotting horizontal ranges on a market trend shouldn't pose as herculean. At all times, market trends show the two main zones; clear support and resistance zones.

Why use the rectangular range strategy?

Rectangular ranges make it easy for traders to find out periods of consolidation easily, and this particular range type also has the most diminutive time frame than other ranges. This feature makes it perfect for day trading. Are you looking forward to faster trading opportunities? Check out the rectangular range strategy.

What is a significant disbenefit of using the rectangular range strategy?

Rectangle ranges could easily mislead a rookie trader who isn't aware that long-term patterns can influence the development of the rectangular shape.

- DIAGONAL RANGE (Price Channels)

Most range traders best in Diagonal ranges as it takes the form of price channels and is very useful in determining common forex chart patterns. A typical diagonal range chart illustrates trendlines, showing whether they are descending or ascending. In addition, Trendlines help identifies breakouts that could occur in range trading.

In the diagonal range type, there are also price fluctuations. The only difference is that it is more controlled as traders will be able to see prices ascending and descending through a trend channel. The channel developed could take any form. It could either be rectangular, narrow or in some cases, very wide. All forms have specific meanings.

WHY WORK WITH DIAGONAL RANGES?

With diagonal ranges, traders will hardly fall victim to a breakout. This range clearly shows that breakouts occur on the opposite end of a trending movement and this gives a heads up, effectively anticipating breakouts and making lots of profit.

Why diagonal ranges might not be the best option?

Although diagonal ranges help predicts breakouts quickly, breakouts don't always show up, some take years, and this makes it tough for diagonal range users to make market price decisions as diagonal range specifically works with breakouts.

- Continuation Range

Continuation range is another strategy heavily patronized by range traders. This type of range has a chart pattern that unfolds within trends. Continuation range is associated with a number of shapes; wedges, flags, Triangles, and pennants. It's basically used to correct trend patterns and each shape it produces depicts the problem associated with a particular price trend. For example, a triangular shape depicts the presence of a tight range during a period of consolidation.

Continuation ranges can also be traded as breakouts, just like diagonal ranges, although continuation ranges depend on the trader's time horizon. Continuation ranges could also occur at any time, either during bearish or bullish periods.

Why work with continuation ranges?

Continuation ranges have the ability to appear more than once in the midst of ongoing market trends. Continuation ranges often lead to quick breakouts, this makes it useful for diagonal range users. Basically, traders who are looking to score a profit within a short period should check out continuation ranges.

Continuation ranges might not be the best option, why?

Due to the fact that this range type occurs within market trends, it's complex to work with as traders will have to account for every variable coming up every minute. A rookie trader should adopt this strategy to avoid confusion in the early stages.

Having discussed the major types of range trading techniques highly patronized by range traders, let's walk through the general strategies that all range traders are expected to work with for better yields:

RANGE IDENTIFICATION

Beginning on the right foot is very important in trading and part of starting up sharp is identifying the trading range. The trading range could be located after a currency must have bounced back from a support area, at least twice in a row. Although it's not a compulsory requirement that highs and lows in market trends should be similar, they should at least be closely related.

A trading range type is identified when highs and lows occur and are pinpointed on the market chart. Although you can't predict the highs and lows of market trends, they happen.

CREATE an Entry

Setting an entry is also as important as identifying a range. You might probably be wondering how to go about setting an entry well, creating an entry involves buying stocks near support levels and reselling when the market is close to resistance levels. To know when the market is in resistance/support levels, make use of indicators. With indicators, you will be able to place trades easily without having to monitor the market trends all day.

Manage Risk

With your range successfully identified and your entry fixed accurately, make sure not to leave out an important aspect of one of the most important aspects of trading, Risk management. This aspect is crucial to your success as a trader. Generally, risk management is important in trading, it's more important when you decide to range trade. Supposing there's a break in the resistance/support level, walking away from a range-based position is the best move, and that's proper risk management.

The best way to ensure your range trading type is risk-averse is by having a stop loss. As a trader, it's advisable that you place stop losses above a high when selling out stocks in the resistance zone of the market trend. You shouldn't forget to invert the process when purchasing a stick during the support period. Also, recall that maximum effort is needed when you introduce the risk management scheme into your range trading.

Unlike scalp trading which embraces the Wild West side of forex, range trading doesn't. Range trading is known to always be on the tame side. Although range trading has faced criticisms claiming it's too basic for this modern market situation, its relevance is still obvious.

High-Frequency Teading (HFT)

HFT is an algorithm trading characterized by swift execution of market trades, handling a large number of trading deals under a short-term investment horizon. HFT leverages unique computers to attain trade execution at the highest possible speed. HFT is a complex algorithm, and it's primarily a device used by big-time investors and companies such as hedge funds and other financial institutions.

HFT is able to spot trends in milliseconds and run trading analyses with its algorithm. With HFT, you can send hundreds of orders in minutes as long as you have the appropriate trigger. Wondering what a High-Frequency Trading technique looks like? Well, here you go:

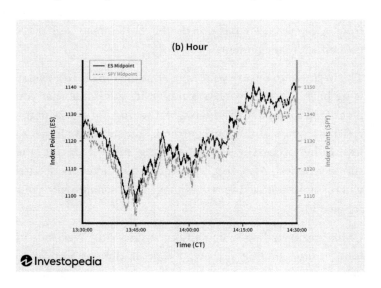

WHAT ARE the Major Benefits of High-Frequency Trading?

- HIGH-FREQUENCY TRADING, alongside high buying rates, allows big-time investors to profit from minor price changes.

In addition, it's a good trading technique for bid-ask spreads.

- HFT's algorithms can successfully scan several markets in a short period. It also opens investors to a wider range of opportunities, including chances to earn from slight price fluctuations for assets.

- PROPONENTS of HFT are confident of the algorithm enhancing liquidity in the market effectively. HFT is said to increase market demand and supply as trades cease to drag and are completed in milliseconds. Increased liquidity results in a significant declination in bid-ask spreads, making the general market more profiting.

- THE LIQUIDITY of a market reduces the risk possibilities, as there will always be an indicator on the other end of the market. Also, as liquidity increases, the seller's price and the buyer's bid will tend to move closer.

- STOP-LOSS ORDER, one of the significant risks associated with HFT, could be easily mitigated as the trader's position remains constant at a particular stage, preventing further losses.

Asides from the stop-loss order, what are the other risks associated with high-frequency trading? Let's find out!

. . .

Risks Associated with HFT

HFT remains a controversial trading technique for some professionals, and among trading regulators and scholars, HFT has little consensus. High-frequency investors seldom hold their portfolio for over 24hours, accumulate funds, and create holdings for a short-term trade type before opting out for liquidation.

As of result of this practice, the risk-reward ratio is always high. The risk-reward ratio of a short-term trader using the HFT technique is much higher than that of a classic investor using the same technique but for long-term trades. An HFT can earn as little as a cent throughout a day and lose as much.

A significant criticism of high-frequency trading is that it doesn't do much in the market other than creating liquidity. HFT protagonists had something to say about this; they said the liquid isn't real because securities don't stay for long in the market. They further explained that before a regular investor purchases a security, it must have been traded a couple of times among high-frequency traders. So, by the time the everyday investor places their orders, there will be no liquidity in the security.

Furthermore, analysis shows that traders using this technique make a profit at the expense of small investors in the market.

Finally, high-frequency trading has been connected to volatility in market uptrends and downtrends. Regulators got hold of some traders using the HFT technique carrying out illegal manipulations like layering and spoofing. These illegal manipulations resulted in market volatility in 2010.

. . .

WHAT ARE the ethics and impact of high-frequency trading?

Regulators and professionals criticize HFT because they believe the technique gives large firms heads-up on trade signals, which unbalances the normal market stability. HFT can also harm other traders that find interest in the long-term type of trading.

HFT critics also have opinions that technologies used in high-frequency trading are one of the significant causes of market volatility. Massive liquidation and some market prices are a result of this technology.

Following these speculations, some European countries are looking to ban HFT to reduce the volatility rate, curb the adverse effect of trading, and ultimately prevent the occurrence of 2010 from happening again.

HFT algorithms have this unique feature of being designed to spark up thousands of orders and terminate them in under a few seconds, creating a momentary fluctuation in price. But, of course, carrying out this kind of operation is considered illegal.

Before we round off this chapter, let's talk about some general tips and rules that guide traders.

GENERAL TRADING RULES and Tips

Here are tips to help you earn more and lose less when trading:

. . .

- CREATE a Plan for your trade

Going into a trade blindly is the worst step one could take as a trader. Always make sure to mark out a plan before trading so occurrences won't come as s shock.

→ TRADE only with the cash you can afford to lose: trading with the cash needed to pay essential bills means gambling, and it's purely against trading ethics.

→ ALSO, you need to be familiar with when to stop trading, cut losses, and pack your profit. This explains why reasons technical analysis is critical. It tells you exactly when to load your profit and stop trading. It also prevents you from being greedy. Being content is the only way one can survive in the market.

- NEVER OVER trade

Newbies usually tend to overtrade, especially in situations where they force themselves in a position of running exchanges at all times. Rookies believe the more you trade, the more you earn. They strongly believe that the only way to be top of your game is by not missing out on any trading activity. However, they most times exist trades they jump into with huge losses. Besides, the compulsory trading fees you seats need to sort out when you trade could eat up your bankroll.

- CUT LOSSES

As discussed earlier in this chapter, cutting your losses is very important during trading activities. Although no one wants to lose, you can't escape it as it's a big part of the game. When trade doesn't turn out well as forecasted, cut your losses almost immediately and be on the look for a totally different opportunity. Provided your investment isn't exhausted, there will always be a second chance. In a nutshell, when things go sideways, cut your losses and move on to the next opportunity. (later in the n-chapter there will be a strategy discussed)

- Trade with the market trend

The market trend comes in waves. The trend shuffled between long and short waves, and the waves sometimes attain top position while a few times they remain down. This is why you should be familiar with technical analysis as a trader. The technical analysis identifies the correct position of the trend and makes sure you go along with it. Many traders make the mistake of selling at the wrong time. They want to profit at quickly as possible without paying attention to the trends. This is very risky since market trends will not always fall in your favor. The best way to trade is to buy before the trend even commences and sell off before it comes to an end. The goal is not to win big; the goal is to win little but consistently.

- Never stop learning

In trading, it's very crucial never to stop learning new things in the trading world. Anytime you suffer losses, write down what resulted in that loss and make sure you never make the same mistake again. People have different mentalities and personalities, so people's learning might be pretty different from one another. In trading, self-experience is the best way to learn; yes! This book can try, but you still have to be practical. You can learn by making mistakes, and you can only make mistakes by making investments and trading. Perseverance and patience are the keys.

2

TECHNICAL ANALYSIS

I'm pretty sure you are looking forward to hearing details about technical analysis and how it could help you boost your returns on trades. Well, here you go!

Technical Analysis is a strategy used to predict the likeliness of developing a trade, stock, or money pair. Technical Analysis is legitimate and should be used by all traders as it centers on the idea of aggregate activities- buying and selling. Using this idea, Technical Analysis accurately mirrors significant data relating to the type of trade you wish to predict, and in the end, doles out a legit review that will make your next transaction successful.

We can't efficiently discuss Technical Analysis without walking through its history. Charles Dow which is one of the pioneers of technical analysis started his life career as a journalist. Dow was born and bred in Sterling, Connecticut, in 1851. As a son of a farmer who was also a journalist, there had always been a high probability that Dow was going to be a journalist. At 21, Dow secured a job as a journalist in Massachusetts with the Springfield Daily Republican. After learning journalism at the Springfield Daily Republican for three years, Dow moved to Rhode Island where he secured a job as a journalist at the Province Star. The Province Star groomed Dow for two years before sending him off to the Province Journal, where he had his breakthrough.

At Province Journal, Dow met George W. Danielson, the editor at that time. Danielson was very impressed with Dow's journals. He adequately commended Dow's method of research and filing reports and offered if he would love to join other professional journalists on a trip to Colorado to carry out research and evaluations on silver mining investment. The trip comprised Dow, professional journalists, and some investors. The investors saw Dow as an observant and talkative young man and gained trust in him. They further invited him to share private information which could be useful in the research and was only for wall street investors to know.

The trip was for just four days, but Dow was able to learned a lot! Part of the major things he learnt from the trip was that with the correct information, one can turn a risky investment into a million-dollar profit. At 29, Dow had completed the life-changing trip at this time, he then moved to New York and became a part of the Street Financial News Bureau. At this bureaucracy, he was the head reporter, so he had every opportunity to go in search of valuable information and compare the effect on the stock price. Been the head reporter at the Street Financial News Bureau was Dow's major achievement at 29.

. . .

At 31, still keeping the good work, Dow partnered with Edward Davis Jones, his friend, and schoolmate at Brown University. Although Davis was a dropout, he never lost focus. Dow saw Davis and a focused journalist with the same vision as his. So together, they established the Dow, Jones & Co Financial news bureau. The establishment was successful and was able to come up with a two-page financial news daily summary for close to six years. In 1889, the Dow, Jones & Co Financial news bureau successfully published its first full-fledged newspaper, the Wall Street Journal. The journal was popular and highly patronized in the 80s' and even till now, people still find it interesting and worth reading. In 1896, which is exactly even years after the newspaper publishment, the Dow Jones Industrial Average (DJIA) was established. To get an average, DJIA comprised 12 companies with a total of 12 closing prices.

DOW TAUGHT us that the market fluctuates and the fluctuations could be predicted by studying indices or price collections of different companies that represent the economy. According to Dow, railroad transportation and the industrials were the core of the economy's growth at that time. In his theory, he said if any of these core engines fail, the economy will most likely fail. Although the industrials could still be one of the core engines of the economy today, railroad transportation is definitely not a core engine as it's not as heavily patronized as it was in the 90s. This shows that Dow's theory of the strongholds of the economy isn't necessarily true today however, the signaling theory works and still persists.

. . .

THE FACT that the signaling theory persists and it's highly acceptable, has a great effect on market trends. If Dow's DJIA starts dropping, news anchors see the drops as significant and start to spread the news that the "market is going down", this makes big-time investors who don't like to take risks suspend their investments, and this suspension would cause the market to dip excessively. Dow's did not only teach us how to study market trends, but he also gave us "Dow theory". Before we proceed, study the technical analysis representation below for better comprehension:

THE DOW THEORY is centered on price movement, which is solely based on 255 editorials that were embedded in one Dow's Street Journal publication. Charles Dow died in 1902, but his theory didn't die as it went through several updates which kept it relevant.

The Dow theory has many ideas, and every one of them has been echoed for years, although this has been in different time frames, that doesn't make the ideas less important. The central idea of the Dow theory is to understand exactly what Charles Dow understood. Dow was convinced that there was a repeating pattern when it comes to stock investment. In his theory, he further explained that the stock investment pattern was directly related to human behavior, and as long as the human behavior doesn't change, the stock pattern will remain the same, following the same pattern. The first step to understanding the whole theory is comprehending this human behavior-stock investment relationship.

Dow Theory: The Six Tenets

My opinion as a trader is that Charles Dow was right in his assumption that patterns do exist. However, his timing of these patterns isn't all that true as other professional traders were able to come up with better patterns. Also, totally accepting that human behavior is directly related to market trend patterns might force you to memorize the time frame of bull periods and this wouldn't be the best as human behavior could change depending on economic, environmental, and most importantly, political conditions. Just like Charles Dow, you will start noticing patterns the more you study market trends. Dow's theory is built on six tenets which are as follows:

- Market trends/stocks follow several cycles simultaneously

First, markets could either follow bullish or bearish movements as these are the only two primary trends markets can take. These primary movements are followed by secondary reactions, which are most times 33% to 67% of the previous market price still following the primary movements. The secondary reaction is then followed by minor movements, which also affect the initial stock price but at a reduced rate compared to the secondary reactions. Imagine a market having a bullish run for eight years with medium swings only in the 6th and 7th years and short swings happening minimally. This is a very crucial observation that could be derived by zooming in and out on the Dow's theory price chart.

Dow Jones Industrial Average (DJIA) short and long-term trend smoothing is an extension of the first tenant of Dow's theory. The smoothing concept explains that not only do we see variations in long and short-term patterns, but patterns could also change entirely when data points are altered. Any time period could be studied using any interval from 60 seconds to 365 days. Using a 4-hour interval as an example, multiple short-term trends smooth out just as seen in a typical 1-hour interval chart. There's more to discuss time intervals when it comes to market trends, but the important takeaway here is that patterns do exist.

Indicators for these patterns are not always accurate mainly because of human behaviors and environmental stimuli. Although environmental stimuli could be studied as they are most times similar, the fact still remains that they are never identical, especially when prior periods are in the study. That might sound a little unclear, re-read again until you understand the idea. When the time interval is changed from 4 hours to something shorter, an entirely different pattern could surface, or we might just obscuring a pattern we've once identified in the 4 hours time interval.

Your choice of time intervals has to do with the level of experience but let's try to simplify a method. Hypothetically, it takes 20 to 30 periods or data points for a particular type of pattern to surface and pose as a trading signal. A day trader could decide to choose a 1 min interval as they most times don't deal with long-term trades, with a one-minute interval, a day trader will most likely get signals every 20 to 30 minutes. On the other hand, long-term traders who have several other businesses to attend to and can't trade within minutes or a few hours tend to use a 24- hour time interval. This time interval type gives a few weeks to days before dropping signals. This is perfect for a busy lifestyle.

You need not worry about making more profits if you trade more like day traders, as long as you make trades using the right signals and make profits any time

you trade. Let's make this more fun by making reference to an occurrence in 2009. This was about an office employee who had bad experiences in the stock market. He then heard about technical analysis and decided to employ the concept in his trading activities. Even with technical analysis, he still couldn't find a good setup in the stock market as he didn't have enough time to study thousands of stock market trends. He was a full-time worker and had other side hustles. He suffered losses for a while until one day when he overheard some of his colleagues talking excitedly about a book that changed their lives. He wasn't into reading books and never saw himself reading a book, but still, at that, he told his wife and family friends about the book his colleagues introduced to him- Hunger Games. Everyone he discussed his encounter with seems excited about it. Sold he decided to conduct research on the book, checking the number of orders the book had secured, and surprisingly, they were a lot. He decided to carry out the huge step of investing in the book's company's stock.

The investment mounted pressure on him as he had to wait for almost a year before noticing a slight price movement. After a while, news broke out that the original movie of the book was a blockbuster hit, so people came in numbers for the book and he made a little fortune. You should also know that he could have lost his investment if the movie was a flop or if he wasn't patient and decided to suspend the investment a few months in. Nonetheless, he made cash from the investment and decided to invest in another book that his colleagues talked about. A few years later, he could conveniently call himself a millionaire. The interesting thing about this narration is that he took some risks, and fortunately, it paid him off. Taking risks could be a lot of fun, but of course, that's if you're not an addict. Sometimes, it's great to have a hunch and to watch your hunch pay off in the long run.

You'll always have this feeling of deserved accomplishment. Although a certain level of information could build your level of confidence, endeavor not to put all your eggs in the same basket. The gentleman we earlier discussed is quite lucky because he made investments in a bull market- when everything was taking a good turn. Supposing he had decided to invest in 2005 or late 2017, it would have been a bad investment for him regardless of the movie's performance. I hope for his sake, he decides to always put the momentum of long- or short-term trends into consideration before making investments.

Before we proceed to the second tenant, have it in mind that the first tenet explains that the first step to a successful trade is deciding if the market is in an uptrend, downtrend, or sideways trend. Once you get this right, everything else will fall into place.

- Long-term primary trends have three phases

These three phases of primary trends follow a particular pattern of behavior. Big-time investors that have the correct information beforehand are usually few in number, and they tend to buy as much as they can sell. However, market prices don't increase because of this as the number of big-time investors who are buying and adding to their shares is a few. The phase where the market price neither spikes nor dips are called the accumulation phase. After this phase is the public participation phase where news and articles start to pop up and people start to catch on, making decisions on whether to buy or sell. Stock prices fluctuated during this phase as trading activities occur. Finally, once the public has either sold or bought stocks, the big-time investors that have bought stocks during the accumulation phase start to sell shares while the rest of the public will most likely experience their profit reduction drastically. This is called the distribution phase.

Economists strongly believe inefficient market hypothesis; they believe that all investors either big-time or small-time, all have access to market information at the same time, and it's almost impossible to beat the market trend. Despite this theory, a pattern still surfaces even before news releases, and people are still able to beat the market to an extent. The market tends to suffer imbalance as not all traders get access to information at the same time. Some get the right signals while others don't. Take cryptocurrencies, for example, a lot of people made heavy cash, and a lot of people also suffered heavy losses. Research showed that most people that suffered losses were holding on to their stock during the third phase (distribution phase) when they were meant to sell out their shares. This doesn't mean this is the accurate explanation for why they suffered losses, this only explains that there was a pattern then and they didn't follow it.

Basically, this second tenet explains that the market trend has three phases; accumulation phase> public participation phase> distribution phase. In a bull market, this cycle is termed a "rally," while in a bear market, it's termed a "sell-off". If all traders had the same information simultaneously, the timing between these phases will be minute. However, there might be no profit to be made.

- Market Averages Must Complement Each Other

As discussed earlier, Dow mentioned the core engines of the economy to be railroad transportation and industrials. If induces for both core factors keep arising, the economy is termed bullish, however, if it happens that both core factors are diverging from each other, the economy could be preparing for a contraction. This third tenet is semi-plausible if utilized without any additions but it's better to understand the concept driving this summary so that its utilization gives a global feel for the markets. Dow's main focuses during his time were the industrials and railroad transportation.

Extrapolated for better comprehension, if we were to takes APPLE's stock as a case study, we will find out that a big portion of their annual revenue comes from China. This makes China a core engine to their market price. Well, supposing the competition in China gained higher grounds or trading activities reduced drastically, China could decide to impose high tax rates on Apple products. This imposition would cause a fall in Apple's annual revenue and thereby leading to a drastic decrease in stock price. The same thing happens when you decide to invest in mortgage companies like Fannie or Freddie. Basically mortgage investment's core engine is the level of interest. When the interest rate increases, mortgages will suffer a drastic reduction in the number of buyers which means fewer people will insure mortgages and this fundamentally causes a decrease in stock prices.

While this might look basic, it could actually be technical sometimes. However, a technical trader is up to the task as he/she would be alert at any slight change in momentum or divergence in trading trends.

- The Stock Market Markdowns Every News

This tenet basically explains that news has a role to play in stock market prices almost instantaneously.it also further explains that a trader could beat a market if able to sell the news. Before you read on, Have this at the back of your mind, Dow's short-term trend lasted for weeks and the long-term trends lasted for decades. Having this kind of time frame during his time makes the whole thing seem natural meaning, News occurs automatically and is priced instantaneously into the stock market. However, this theory isn't so true for all kinds of trade trends especially short-term trades. This tenet perfectly explains your perspective as a trader. But in this case, perspective is the time frame you chose. The two examples discussed earlier where we made reference to Apple securing a big-time annual revenue decrease and Fannie and Freddie's interest rate stock market increase are termed unexpected news. You're probably wondering what unexpected news is. Well, is a 2-way thing, news can either be expected or unexpected. Unexpected news is known to cause a rapid market action that will hardly be caught in a long-term frame trade. Charles Dow's focus was mainly on unexpected news.

If Apple's response to the increase in the competition was to cut its revenue forecast, the news will probably be delayed, taking hours and potentially weeks before the stock price reached a bottom level. However, investors who had earlier sold their stock will make big bags during this period. Nobody might suffer any loss as investors who also followed the revenue forecasts of the competition in China would have sold their stock just before the news is released. You should also have in mind that during this period, Apple's stock would be in a downward momentum but the rate of fall wouldn't be significant at least before the news shows up. In a nutshell, does the stock market really markdown all news? Yes! Absolutely. In the sense that, there's always a big change in stock price after news has been released, but no in the sense that investors can still make a profit from the market even after the news has been released. Professional traders testified that it's quite hard to adequately monitor every change in the core engines of market prices and if you're a part-time trader, it could even be harder to churn out profit immediately the news is out.

Professional traders also embrace the use of stop losses but this solely depends on the volatility rate of the stock market. Stop losses tend to have fixed prices in some events especially in situations where unexpected news is released. It's advisable to avoid stop losses during this period as it could affect your investment. To adequately monitor a stock market's volatility rate, you could make use of indicators. The use of indicators will further be discussed in this book, keep reading. I've once used the Average True Range indicator and from my experience, I wouldn't say it's a bad option as I was able to manage my losses and protect my investments. This 4th tenet is also an important reminder that for whatsoever reason, retirement accounts are not the best accounts to utilize to stop losses and this is because, when the economy crashes, retirement accounts tend to lose all potential gains that they've made in years. Although stop losses are widely used by technical traders in the trading world, you can still suffer losses if not used the right way.

- Market Trends and Volume work together

Market prices fluctuate with little changes in volume. A change in volume occurs when a minority of investors are going through bearish or bullish runs. Changes in volume could alter the trend if the majority of big-time investors are not on board. Have it at the back of your mind that a change in volume is relative and when studying changes in volume, you're not studying the absolute volume but the average volume. Sounds a bit confusing? Read again to comprehend better.

- Trends Persists Unless Altered

This tenet is basically laying emphasis on the obvious. It's logical to say Dow tried imitating the popular baseball player Yogi Berra who is popularly known for quoting the most obvious statements. Well, one could say Down was being insightful in this last tenet. Are you familiar with Newton's First Law of Motion? If yes, it will be very easy for you to understand this tenet. The Law states that an object will continue to be in its resting state unless a force acts on it. Now let's see how It's related to Dow's tenet. In technical analysis generally, a market trend persists provided all determining factors are constant. Trends don't last forever and this is the only reason why there could be a change in the trend without any factor been altered. There are only three types of market trends; the downtrend, uptrend, and horizontal trend.

In short-term trades, the trends tend to change frequently, an uptrend could at any point have a horizontal or a downtrend. This is a very simple illustration except for where the formation of new trends happens and technical investors are stuck on how to identify it. Most times it's advisable to make use of more than one indicator. Using two or three indicators increasing your level of confidence as two indicators signaling a trend reversal is hardly a wrong prediction. There's this popular saying during the 90s that if more than one indicators agree, it means you're probably too late for a trade or a stock price has undergone a change. One crucial observation you should always look out for when dealing with indicators is that there are a lot of momentum indicators that can successfully pinpoint trade reversal signals when using a long-term trend as a reference point. Sometimes, technical analysts even find it difficult to tell if a trend reversal is just a correction in alignment with a primary trend or a reversal of the primary trend. The distinction between different types of trends hasn't been accurately identified but with the right indicators and frequent practice, you'll secure more wins than losses in your predictions.

Technical analysis is a trading technique that all traders should use for the bulk of their trading activities. You should also make use of fundamentalism analysis but try to make sure it's not the major technique used in your trading. You could decide to dedicate a small portion of your portfolio to the fundamental analysis technique. Fundamental analysis is regarded as more theoretical than practical as it deals with the company's fundamentals, statements, modus operandi, and so on. Technical analysis doesn't really engage in finding out these details. It has to do with the strict analysis of stock price movement without regard to fundamentals. Technical analysis makes traders understand that even if a company has stellar profit margins, a high growth rate, or a low debt rate if they have a large number of stock sellers, the market price will decrease.

With an adequate understanding of the technical analysis concept, you can study price fluctuations in relation to the purchasing power of stocks, this is called studying the "momentum" of trading. Technical analysis also makes traders understand the concept of buying at low rates and selling at high rates. It further explains the concept saying it works best when a trader uses fundamental analysis, only a few stocks are at stake, and if the trader is willing to operate a long-term trade type. Technical analysis also explains that the best way is successful using momentum trading is by making sure you're not the last person to sell momentum stocks at any point. This is because a delay in-stock purchase could render you profitless as every other trader would have sold their stocks and the market price would have reduced drastically, below the price you're supposed to realize a profit from. In the next chapter, we will be discussing how to monitor price fluctuations from different market charts, this will help limit your losses at times when you make bad predictions. Technical analysis ensures that all traders have more rights than wrongs in their trading activities. Being at least 60% right and 40% wrong means you'll make a profit at the end of the trading year. That's the goal of technical analysis! Check out the next chapter so you'll get better at trading markets charts. I'm sure you can't wait.

3

CHART READING AND ITS RELEVANCE IN TRADING

I'm sure you learned a whole lot from the previous chapter well, you should see this chapter as a progression. In this chapter, our main focus will be chart reading and its importance in trading.

As a brokerage account owner, one of your privileges is free to access to stock's advanced chart. In these charts, you will be allowed to introduce technical indicators automatically, inputting trendlines will also come easy and you'll also be able to compare price charts with one another. Prosperous traders have some principles that build their knowledge about trading. Learning these principles will go a long way in also building your knowledge in trading.

The 3 Universal Principles of Trading

The first principle you need to adopt is spending at least half an hour daily checking through financial news. Adoption of this principle comes easy with online platforms, some of these platforms include:

- https://www.economist.com/finance-and-economics/
- https://finance.yahoo.com/

Besides these major online platforms, there are also several applications online which provide financial news. Applications like the MarketWatch app, CNBC finance app, and the popular Wall Street Journal.

The second principle is to be conversant of price fluctuations of stocks and ETFs that you find interest in. The point here's you must be optimistic about these stocks because optimism will help compound your knowledge as you'll want to follow up on every step, trading more about the stock within the ETF that you find interest in.

The third principle which is the central idea of this chapter is spending a few minutes daily going through price charts of previously completed trades and charts showing stock price fluctuations. Closely monitor the charts and try to identify patterns, and practice predicting price movements from the patterns you identify. Online platforms like tradingview.com and stockcharts.com have active groups of rookie traders who go public with their technical analyses and predictions. You should flow with these rookies and get to find out if they come about the same pattern you've identified. These platforms are time-consuming be wary of them, but make sure you derive analyses of different traders from the platform so as to conduct proper comparisons.

. . .

With these three principles, you will get to discover that price fluctuations' comprehension and impact will continue to increase over time. Also, be wary of the fact that you'll find several types of technical analyses that you'll prefer over time, and this is regarded as a favorable result because it will be easy for you to explore different trading techniques and read charts perfectly, it will basically mean more money for you!

Core Elements of Trading

Starting your journey in chart reading, you will need to come to a conclusion whether you prefer studying stick charts using a Logarithmic scale or an Arithmetic scale.

Chart reading using the Arithmetic scale is designed in such a way that the y-axis comprises absolute numbers such that for instance, an increase in price from $20- $30 and another price increase from $60-$70 will both spike up the y-axis by $10 which is the difference in both cases.

For a Logarithmic scale, the y-axis comprises a percentage change. Here, a $10 difference from $20-$30 is bound to show a 100% increase on the vertical axis while a similar dollar change from $60-$70 will specifically only show a 20% increase on the vertical axis (y-axis).

Having picked the scale type that works with you best, you will then proceed to decide what chart type is best for the scale type you chose. Generally, there are four chart types used in trading and all these chart types work in both bulk and bear seasons. The different chart types include:

- Bar chart
- Line chart
- Point and figure chart
- Candlestick charts

The next move is switching to multiple windows. For traders who fancy swing trading, it's advisable to use the 12 hours, 24 hours, window types. Find out if you're dealing with a downtrend or an uptrend. The best way to find out what kind of trend you're working with is by monitoring the peaks. When a new peak that just appeared is lower than the old peak, it's regarded as 'lower highs'. Lower highs indicate downtrends. A stronger conviction is noticed when price fluctuations are called downtrends, the opposite of what is termed as higher highs, or uptrends or higher lows.

AFTER THE IDENTIFICATION of uptrends and downtrends, the next move is drawing the resistance and support level by making use of progressing averages, trendlines, or static price levels. This isn't a difficult task as you could handle it mentally in under a few seconds. It's at this stage that you'll make use of your indicators, and be more conversant of four elements which include; divergence, false breakouts, breakouts, and convergence.

In trading, a divergence is when the price of a commodity and its indicator is moving in different directions.

Convergence, on the other hand, is when the price of the commodity and its indicator is moving in a similar direction.

Breakouts are divided into bull and bear breakouts as both seasons have different interpretations of what breakouts actually mean.

A bull breakout is when prices of stocks break ridiculously above the resistance level. A bull breakout is usually followed by an increase in volume which in return ultimately increases the stock's volatility and its percentage profit.

A bear breakout is very different from a bull breakout. Here, the price breaks below the support level and the break is usually followed by an increase in stock volume.

YOU'RE PROBABLY WONDERING why they are called breakouts well, they are called breakouts because upcoming resistance and support levels are confirmed too long ago that the market tends to run without noticing its impact. A major cause of delay in breakouts showing up in market trends is the lack of sufficient stock volume and price change to cause trade to shut down their market positions, breakouts like this without sufficient momentum are called false breakouts. False breakouts are common in trading gaps.

HAVING DISCUSSED the major elements of typical trading charts, let's now bring you to understanding how a chart works, from the patterns, components, bear rising, bullish rising, and lots more. To do this, let's divert our focus mainly on candlestick charts.

Understanding the Basics of Trading Charts

To adequately understand the basics of candlestick charts, we will be buttressing on these subheadings:

- Candlestick components
- Candlestick against Bar Charts
- Basic Patterns in Candlestick Charts
- Bearish Engulfing Pattern
- Bullish Engulfing Pattern
- Bearish Evening Star
- Bearish Harami

Candlestick charts began in Japan about a century ago just before the West originated the bar charts. During the 1700s, Homma, a Japanese trader found that there was a connection between stock prices and Rice's organic market, he also discovered that the business sectors at that time were hugely impacted by how traders felt.

CANDLESTICK CHART WAS of utmost importance at that time because it clearly showed the feeling of these traders by outwardly presenting the price fluctuations with several tones. Traders now and then, utilized candlestick charts to settle on trading choices which are reliant on reoccurring signals that support predictions of the price's course during movement. Well, this is not the only benefit of the candlestick chart, other benefits include:

• With Candlestick trends, investors can easily predict price fluctuations using patterns recorded in the past.

- With the ability to show up to four price focuses; low, high, close, and open, for as long as the investors want to know, you can hardly go wrong as a trader using candlestick.

- Most trade calculations are dependent on similar price data shown on a typical candlestick chart.

- Just as we discussed earlier, trading is controlled to an extent by feeling. The feeling could be read in candle charts

CANDLESTICK COMPONENTS

Just like a bar trend, a candle depicts the market's high, low, close, and open price for trades in the afternoon. The candlestick comprises a broad part regarded as the "real body."

This real body explains the stock price range between the market's open and close for daily trades. At the long when the real body is dark, the candlestick is trying to explain that the nearby is lower than the market's open. But when the real body is empty, it implies that the nearby is higher than the market's open.

Another unique property of candlestick is that investors are allowed to modify the real body shadings in their trading stage. For instance, a down candle could be depicted as red instead of the standard color, red. An up candlestick on the other hand could be depicted as green instead of the standard white color. A typical candlestick chart is represented as:

. . .

Candlestick Against Bar Charts

Above and beneath a typical real body are entities called the "wicks" or "shadows." The wicks have just one function, to show trade prices at both high and low levels. On the off probability that the upper wick on a light beneath is short, it depicts that the open for that particular trading session was close to the high of the day.

A short upper wick on an up day depicts that the nearby was really close to the high. Basically the connection between the days open, close, high, low, determines the final look of the candlestick on a daily basis. Real bodies can either be dark or white which shows emptiness and they could also be long or short. Wicks can also either be long or short.

Bar trends and candlestick charts both have data in common, but they do this in an alternative way. Candle charts are more visible basically because of the shading which the price bars have and the thickness of the real bodies. The real bodies are best at figuring out the difference between the nearby and the open.

Basic Patterns in Candlestick Charts

Here and their movement of stock prices is the perfect way to describe candlestick patterns. While price fluctuations are seen most times as random, at several scenarios they reconstruct pretend that traders make use of them for drawing out analysis for trading purposes. There are several candlestick patterns. Below is a list of them, you can kick off with it.

Patterns are divided into bearish and bullish. For bullish patterns, they are very essential in trading activities because they show the probability of the stock price rising, while the bearish on the other hand. Indicates a stock price fall. However, you should always have in mind that these patterns don't work every day. They are no form of assurance, they just give signals for price fluctuations.

Bearish Engulfing Pattern

This pattern is known for creating uptrends in situations where the investor decided to draft buyers. This bearish engulfing pattern activity is reflected by a long real body designed red, engulfing another real body designed with green. This pattern shows that investors are in charge of the market and the market prices could keep going down.

Bullish Engulfing Pattern

This type of pattern shows up when the purchasers dominate the sellers. A bullish engulfing pattern is reflected in the market trend by a real body designed in green engulfing another real body designed in red. With bulls controlling the market, the price will definitely head higher.

Bearish Evening Star

An evening star is regarded as a fixing chart. It's differentiated by the last light in signal opening under the earlier day's real body. This real body just like other real bodies can either be green or red. The ultimate candle rounds off deep into the real body of the initial candle two days prior. This pattern depicts a decrease in the pace of the purchasers and afterward, stock sellers are seen dominating the market.

Bearish Harami

A bearish harami is a real body designed in red found inside another real body that was formed prior. The bearish harami pattern isn't complicated to follow up on, however, it needs close monitoring. The pattern basically depicts hesitations with respect to purchasers. In a situation whereby the price proceeds to the top a few moments later, all may, in any scenario, be okay with the market's uptrend, however, a candlestick faced downsides follow the bearish pattern indicates a further step.

If you're looking to be a successful trader, learning how to read stock charts has to be one of your major goals. Even professional traders who make use of technical analysis and fundamental analysis to carry out trading activities still need a sound knowledge of how to go about tame aging charts as you can't use an indicator either make swift trades without knowing how to interpret a stock chart!

4

TREND REVERSALS: A TREND BECOMING AN OPPOSITE TREND

An important skill you need to acquire as a trader, either as a rookie or veteran, is the ability to predict accurately, period of successful breakouts or reversals. This chapter basically explains the concept of trend reversals, and how having a sound knowledge about them helps you as a trader. Recall from previous chapters that we made mention of every trend bar being a breakout, we also mentioned that on top of bull and bear trend bars, there are investors who are always willing to buy or sell regardless of the trend bar's state or nature. There are two types of traders when it comes to breakouts, those that will place stakes on the belief that a breakout will be successful, and traders that will invest on the trend bar yielding a reversal rather than a breakout. Here's is a typical example of an opposite trend

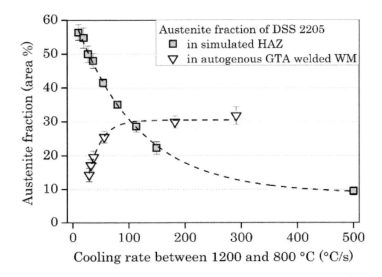

A REVERSAL OCCURRING IMMEDIATELY after a single bar on a typical 15 minutes chart is most likely a reversal that happened along several bars on a 1-minute chart, and a reversal happening over more than 10 bars is most likely a one-bar reversal happening on a 120-minute chart. Here's what a bar trend looks like.

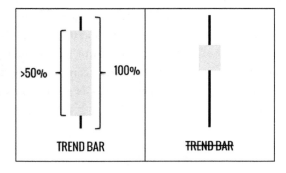

This bar trend is similar on all time frames, either in a single bar or multiple bars scenarios. OMG an edge over your trades means possessing the ability to figure out what direction the market will go after a breakout happens or develops. Of all trading setups, reversal setups are the most common, and this is because most trend bars are breakouts and will all be most likely be followed by a trial to either make the breakout reverse or fail.

In an attempt to make a breakout take a reverse, the reversal attempt must be stronger than the breakout, this is basically what is needed for a successful reversal. However, if the reversal attempt is not as strong, the process will not be successful and the reversal attempt will be seen as the inception of a flag in the new trend. Let's try to explain this using an example. Hypothetically, let's assume there's a bull break out of a certain trading range and the bulk spike comprises two huge bulk trend bars with little tails, and the consecutive bar is a bear Doji bar, that Doji bar is the attempt we discussed that is used to cause a breakout failure or reversal into a bear trend. Given that the breakout is a lot stronger than the Doji bar which is the reversal attempt, there's a high possibility that there are much more buyers than sellers just beneath the bear bar and that the entry bar which represents the short will turn out to become a distinct breakout pull-back. So basically, the reversal attempt wouldn't be succeeding but rather, it will turn out to be the inception of a bull flag following another leg up.

However, if the strength of the reversal is sufficient to deal with the breakout, there's every possibility that the breakout will fail and the market trend will experience a reversal. In a nutshell, it's simply a matter of more breakout strength, more possibility for reversal failure, resulting in a pullback setup.

Trend reversals can't be discussed comprehensively without talking about institutional trading. This leads us to the concept of institutional trading.

INSTITUTIONAL TRADING IS CARRIED out by computers and sometimes discretionary traders, institutional trading has also made us see the importance of computer programming in trading. Most institutions center their trading activities on basics or sometimes technical information, some can even decide to combine the two in trading activities. Basically, discretionary traders base decisions they come up with primarily on information basics, while computer program trades are centered on technical data. In the late 20th century, one institution actively running a huge program had the capability to change market positions. Changing market positions, the program would also produce a microchannel, most traders back then, saw this as a sign that a program was in action. In this present day, several trading days have more than a dozen micro-channels embedded in Emini, and many more have thousands of contracts traded. With the Emini currently around 1200, that corresponds to $6 billion, and is larger than a single institution would trade for a single small trade. This means that a single institution cannot move the market very far or for very long and that all movement on the chart is caused by many institutions trading in the same direction at the same time. Also, HFT computers analyze every tick and are constantly placing trades all day long. Below is a graph representing institutional trading:

When they detect a program, many will scalp in the direction of the program, and they will often account for most of the volume while the micro channel (program) is progressing.

The institutions that are trading largely on technical information cannot move the market in one direction forever because at some point the market will appear as offering value to the institutions trading on fundamentals. If the technical institutions run the price up too high, fundamental institutions and other technical institutions will see the market as being at a great price to sell out of longs and to initiate shorts, and they will overwhelm the bullish technical trading and drive the market down. When technical trading creates a bear trend, the market at some point will be clearly cheap in the eyes of fundamental and other technical institutions. The buyers will come in and overwhelm the technical institutions responsible for the sell-off and reverse the market up. Trend reversals on all time frames always happen at support and resistance levels, because technical traders and programs look for them as areas where they should stop pressing their bets and begin to take profits, and many will also begin to trade in the opposite direction. Since they are all based on mathematics, computer algorithms, which generate 70 percent of all trading volume and 80 percent of institutional volume, know where they are.

Also, institutional fundamental traders pay attention to obvious technical factors. They see major support and resistance on the chart as areas of value and will enter trades in the opposite direction when the market gets there. The programs that trade on value will usually find it around the same areas because there is almost always significant value by any measure around major support and resistance. Most of the programs make decisions based on price, and there are no secrets. When there is an important price, they all see it, no matter what logic they use. The fundamental traders (people and machines) wait for value and commit heavily when they detect it. They want to buy when they think that the market is cheap and sell when they believe it is expensive.

FOR EXAMPLE, if the market is falling, but it's getting to a price level where the institutions feel like it is getting cheap, they will appear out of nowhere and buy aggressively. This is seen most dramatically and often during opening reversals (the reversals can be up or down and are discussed in the section on trading the open later in this exquisite book). The bears will buy back their shorts to take profits and the bulls will buy to establish new longs. No one is good at knowing when the market has gone far enough, but most experienced traders and programs are usually fairly confident in their ability to know when it has gone too far.

Because the institutions are waiting to buy until the market has become clearly oversold, there is an absence of buyers in the area above a possible bottom, and the market is able to accelerate down to the area where they are confident that it is cheap. Some institutions rely on programs to determine when to buy and others are discretionary. Once enough of them buy, the market will usually turn up for at least a couple of legs and about 10 or more bars on whatever time frame chart where this is happening. While it is falling, institutions continue to short all the way down until they determine that it has reached a likely target and it is unlikely to fall any further, at which point they take profits.

THE MORE OVERSOLD the market becomes, the more of the selling volume is technically based because fundamental traders and programs will not continue to short when they think that the market is cheap and should soon be bought. The relative absence of buyers as the market gets close to a major support level often leads to an acceleration of the selling into the support, usually resulting in a sell vacuum that sucks the market below the support in a climactic sell-off, at which point the market reverses up sharply. Most support levels will not stop a bear trend (and most resistance levels will not stop a bull trend), but when the market finally reverses up, it will be at an obvious major support level, as a long-term trend line. The bottom of the sell-off and the reversal up is usually on very heavy volume. As the market is falling, it has many rallies up to resistance levels and sell-offs down to support levels along the way, and each reversal takes place when enough institutions determine that it has gone too far and is offering value for a trade in the opposite direction. When enough institutions act around the same level, a major reversal takes place.

THERE ARE fundamental and technical ways to determine support. For example, it can be estimated with calculations, like what the S&P 500 price-earnings multiple should theoretically be, but these calculations are never sufficiently precise for enough institutions to agree. However, traditional areas of support and resistance are easier to see and therefore more likely to be noticed by many institutions, and they more clearly define where the market should reverse. In both the crashes of 1987 and 2008–2009, the market collapsed down to slightly below the monthly trend line and then reversed up, creating a major bottom. The market will continue up, with many tests down, until it has gone too far, which is always at a significant resistance level. Only then can the institutions be confident that there is clear value in selling out of longs and selling into shorts. The process then reverses down.

The fundamentals (the value in buying or selling) determine the overall direction, but the technology determines the actual turning points. The market is always probing for value, which is an excess, and is always at support and resistance levels. Reports and news items at any time can alter the fundamentals (the perception of value) enough to make the market trend up or down for minutes to several days. Major reversals lasting for months are based on fundamentals and begin and end at support and resistance levels. This is true of every market and every time frame.

It is important to realize that the news will report the fundamentals as still bullish after the market has begun to turn down from a major top, and still bearish after it has turned up from a major bottom. Just because the news still sees the market as bullish or bearish does not mean that the institutions still do. Trade the charts and not the news. Price is truth and the market always leads the news. In fact, the news is always the most bullish at market tops and most bearish at market bottoms. The reporters get caught up in the euphoria or despair and search for pundits who will explain why the trend is so strong and will continue much longer. They will ignore the smartest traders, and probably do not even know who they are. Those traders are interested in making money, not news, and will not seek out the reporters. When a reporter takes a cab to work and the driver tells him that he just sold all of his stocks and mortgaged his house so that he could buy gold, the reporter gets excited and can't wait to find a bullish pundit to put on the air to confirm the reporter's profound insight in the gold bull market. "Just think, the market is so strong that even my cabbie is buying gold! Everyone will therefore sell all of their other assets and buy more, and the market will have to race higher for many more months!" To me, when even the weakest traders finally enter the market, there is no one left to buy.

The market needs a greater fool who is willing to buy higher so that you can sell out with a profit. When there is no one left, the market can only go one way, and it is the opposite of what the news is telling you. It is difficult to resist the endless parade of persuasive professorial pundits on television who are giving erudite arguments about how gold cannot go down and in fact will double again over the next year. However, you have to realize that they are there for their own self-aggrandizement and for entertainment. The network needs entertainment to attract viewers and advertising dollars. If you want to know what the institutions are really doing, just look at the charts. The institutions are too big to hide and if you understand how to read charts, you will see what they are doing and where the market is heading, and it is usually unrelated to anything that you see on television.

A SUCCESSFUL TREND reversal is a change from a bull market to a bear market or from a bear market to a bull market, and the single most important thing to remember is that most trend reversal attempts fail. A market has inertia, which means that it has a strong propensity to continue what it has been doing and a strong resistance to change. The result is that there is really no such thing as a trend reversal pattern. When there is a trend, all patterns are continuation patterns, but occasionally one will fail. Most technicians will label that failure as a reversal pattern, but since most of the time it fails as a reversal and the trend continues, it is really more accurately thought of as just a continuation pattern. A trend is like a huge ship that takes a lot of force applied over time to change its direction. There usually has to be some increase in two-sided trading before traders in the other direction can take control, and that two-sided trading is a trading range. Because of this, most reversal patterns are trading ranges, but you should expect the breakout from the trading range to be in the direction of the trend because that is what happens in about 80 percent of cases. Probably wondering what a breakout looks like, well, here you go:

Sometimes the breakout will be in the opposite direction or the with-trend breakout will quickly fail and then reverse. When those events happen, most traders will label the trading range as a reversal pattern, like a double top, a head and shoulders, or a final flag. All of the reversal patterns listed in Part I can lead to a trend in the opposite direction, but they can also simply lead to a trading range, which is more likely to be followed by a trend resumption. In this case, the reversal pattern is just a bull flag in a bull trend or a bear flag in a bear trend. When a trend reverses, the reversal can be sharp and immediate and have a lot of conviction early on, or it can happen slowly over the course of a dozen or more bars.

Sharp Trend Reversal

When trend reversal happens slowly, the market usually appears to be forming just another flag, but the pullback continues to grow until at some point the with-trend traders give up and there is a breakout in the countertrend direction.

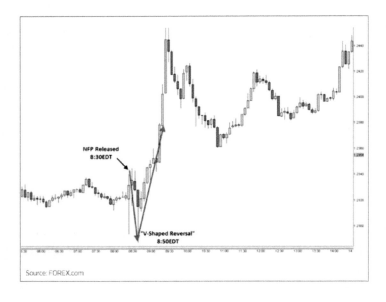

For example, assume that there is a bear trend that is beginning to pull back and it forms a low 1 setup, but the market immediately turns up after the signal triggers. It then triggers a low 2 entry and that, too, fails within a bar or so. At this point, assume that either the market breaks out of the top of the bear flag or it has one more push up, triggering a wedge bear flag, the entry fails, and then the market has a breakout to the upside. A reversal at some point makes the majority of traders believe that the always-in position has reversed, and this almost always requires some kind of breakout. At this point, there is a new trend, and traders reverse their mindset. When a bull trend reverses to a bear trend, they stop buying above bars on stops and buying below bars on limit orders and begin selling above bars on limit orders and selling below bars on stops. When a bear trend reverses to a bull trend, they stop selling below bars on stops and selling above bars on limit orders and begin buying above bars on stops and buying below bars on limit orders.

EVERY TREND IS CONTAINED within a channel, which is bordered by a trend line and a trend channel line, even though the channel may not be readily apparent on a quick look at the chart. The single most important rule in these books is that you should never be thinking about trading against a trend until after there has been a breakout of the channel, which means a break beyond a significant trend line. Also, you should take a reversal trade only if there is a strong signal bar. You need evidence that the other side is strong enough to have a chance of taking control. And even then, you should still be looking for with-trend trades because, after this first countertrend surge, the market almost always goes back in the direction of the trend to test the old trend extreme. Only rarely is the trend line break on such strong momentum that the test won't be tradable for at least a scalp. If the market fails again around the price of the old extreme, then it has made two attempts to push through that level and failed, and whenever the market tries twice to do something and fails, it usually tries the opposite. It is after this test of the old extreme that you should look for countertrend swing trades and only if there is a good setup on the reversal away from the old extreme.

IT IS VERY important to distinguish a reversal trade from a countertrend scalp. A reversal trade is one where an always-in flip is likely. A countertrend scalp is not a reversal trade; it usually has a bad trader's equation and most often forms within a channel. Channels always look like they are about to reverse, suckering traders into countertrend trades using stop entries. These traders soon get trapped and have to cover with a loss. For example, if there is a bull channel, it will usually have a reasonable-looking bear reversal or inside bar after the breakout to every new high. Here's what a countertrend scalp looks like:

Beginners will see that there is enough room to the moving average for a short scalp and will short on a stop below the bar. They will lose money on 70 percent or more of their countertrend scalps, and their average loser will be larger than their average winner. They take the shorts because they are eager to trade and most of the buy signals look weak, often forcing traders to buy within a few ticks of the top of the channel. The countertrend setups often have good-looking signal bars, which convince traders that they can finesse a short scalp while waiting for a good-looking buy setup. They see all of the prior bear reversal bars and pullbacks as signs of building selling pressure, and they are right. However, most short scalps will end up being just micro-sell vacuums, where the market is getting sucked down to a support level, like around the bottom of the channel, or below a minor higher low. Once there, the strong bulls begin to buy aggressively. Many take profits at the new high, creating the next sell signal, which will fail like all of the earlier ones. High-frequency trading firms pay minuscule commissions and can profitably trade for one or two ticks, but you cannot. Although there are good-looking reversal bars, these are not tradable reversals, and traders should not take them. As long as the signal is not good enough to flip the always-in direction to short, only trade in the direction of the trend. The institutions are buying below the lows of those who sell signal bars. If you want to trade while the channel is forming, you either have to buy with limit orders below prior bars, like the institutions, or buy above high 2 signal bars, which is where the bears usually buy back their losing shorts. However, this is difficult for many traders, because they can see that the channel has a lot of two-sided trading and know that buying at the top of a channel, where there is a lot of two-sided trading, is an approach that often has only a marginally positive trader's equation.

A TREND REVERSAL, or simply a reversal, is not necessarily an actual trend reversal because the term implies that the market is changing from one behavior to any opposite behavior.

TRADING RANGE BEHAVIOR is arguably the opposite of trending behavior, so if a trading range breaks out into a trend, that is a reversal of the behavior of the market, but it is more commonly described as a breakout. A pullback is a small trading range and a small trend against the larger trend, and when the pullback ends, that minor trend reverses back into the direction of the major trend. Most trend reversals end up as higher time frame pullbacks in the trend, which means that most end up as large trading ranges; however, some become strong, persistent trends in the opposite direction. Even when the reversal leads to a trading range, the reversal entry will usually go far enough to be a swing trade.

MOST TREND REVERSAL attempts do not result in a strong, opposite trend and instead lead to trading ranges. Strictly speaking, the behavior has reversed into an opposite type of price action (from one-sided trading to two-sided trading), but the trend has not reversed into an opposite trend. A trader never knows in advance if there will be a reversal into a new trend, and a reversal into a trading range often looks the same as a reversal into a new trend for dozens of bars. Because of this, a trader does not know until much later whether there has been a reversal into the opposite trend or just a transition into a trading range. This is why the probability of most trades, where the reward is many times greater than the risk, is so small at the outset. As the moves become more certain, the reward gets smaller, because there are fewer ticks left to the move, and the risk gets larger because the theoretically ideal stop for a swing trade goes beyond the start of the most recent spike (below the most recent higher low in a bull or above the most recent lower high in a bear, which can be far away). From a trader's perspective, it does not matter because traders are going to trade the reversal the same way, whether it evolves into a strong new trend or simply into a couple of large countertrend legs. Yes, they would make more money from a huge swing that does not come back to their breakeven stops, but they can still make a lot of money if the market stalls and simply becomes a large trading range. However, in a trading range, traders will usually make more money if they look for scalps rather than swings. In a true trend reversal, the new trend can go a long way and traders should swing most of their position.

IF THE MARKET does reverse into an opposite trend, the new trend may be either protracted or limited to a single bar. The market may also simply drift sideways after a bar or two, and then trend again later, either up or down. Many technicians will not use the term reversal except in hindsight, after a series of trending highs and lows has formed. However, this is not useful in trading because waiting for that to occur will result in a weaker trader's equation, since a significant pullback (a greater drawdown) in that new trend becomes more likely the longer the trend has been in effect. Once a trader is initiating trades in the opposite direction to the trend, that trader believes that the trend has reversed even though the strict criteria have not yet been met. For example, if traders are buying in a bear trend, they believe that the market will likely not trade even a single tick lower; otherwise, they would wait to buy. Since they are buying with the belief that the market will go higher, they believe the trend is now upward and therefore a reversal has taken place, at least on a scale large enough for the trade to be profitable.

Many technicians will not accept this definition, because it does not require some basic components of a trend to exist. Most would agree on two requirements for a trend reversal. The first is an absolute requirement: the move has to break a trend line from the prior trend so that the old trend channel has been broken. The second requirement happens most of the time but is not required: after the trend line break, the market comes back and successfully tests the extreme of the old trend. Rarely, there can be a climactic reversal that has a protracted initial move and never comes close to testing the old extreme.

THE SEQUENCE IS the same for any reversal. Every trend is in a channel and when there is a move that breaks the trend line, the market has broken out of the channel. This breakout beyond the trend line is followed by a move back in the direction of the trend. The trend traders want this to be a failed reversal attempt and for the old trend to resume. If they are right, the new trend channel will usually be broader and less steep, which indicates some loss of momentum. This is natural as a trend matures. They see this trend line break as simply leading to another flag that will be followed by an extension of the trend.

The countertrend traders want this reversal back in the direction of the old trend, after the breakout, to be a breakout test and then be followed by at least a second leg against the old trend. In a successful breakout, instead of resuming the trend, the test reverses once more and the test becomes a breakout pullback in the new trend, or at least in a larger correction. For example, in the breakout above the bear trend line in a bear trend, at some point, the reversal will attempt to fail and then sell off to a lower low, a double bottom, or a higher low, which is the test of the bear low. If that test is successful, that test becomes a breakout pullback in the breakout above the bear trend line and the new bull trend resumes for at least one more leg. When the reversal up results in a reversal into a new trend, the rally that broke above the bear trend line is when the bulls began to take control over the market, even if the pullback from this bull breakout falls to a lower low. Most traders will see the lower low as the start of the bull trend, but the bulls often take control during the spike that breaks above the bear trend line. It does not matter if you say that the bull began at the bottom of the bull spike or at the bottom of the lower low reversal, because you trade the market the same. You look to buy as the market is reversing up from the lower low (or double bottom or higher low). The rally that follows could become a large two-legged correction, the start of a trading range, or a new bull trend. No matter what the end result is, the bulls have a good chance of a profitable trade. If the test is unsuccessful, the market will continue down into a new bear leg and traders have to look for another breakout above the new bear channel and then another test of the new bear low before looking to buy a bottom. The opposite is true when there is a bull trend that has a bear spike below the bull trend line, and then a higher high, double top, or lower high pullback from the breakout. The bears began to take control over the market during the spike. The test of the bull high, even if it exceeds the old high, is still simply a pullback from the initial bear breakout below the bull trend line.

Once there has been a strong countertrend move, the pullback will be a test for both the bulls and the bears. For example, suppose there was a strong downward move in a bull market, and the move broke through a trend line that had held for 20 to 40 bars; it then continued down for 20 bars and carried well below the 20-bar moving average, and even beneath the low of the last higher low of the bull trend; in this case, the bears have demonstrated considerable strength. Once this first leg down exhausts itself, bears will begin to take partial profits, and bulls will begin to reinstate their longs. Both will cause the market to move higher, and both bulls and bears will watch this move very carefully. Because the down leg was so strong, both the bulls and the bears believe that its low will likely be tested before the market breaks out into a new high. Therefore, as the market rallies, if there is not strong momentum up, the new bulls will start to take profits, and the bears will become aggressive and add to their shorts.

ALSO, the bulls who held through the sell-off will use this rally to begin to exit their longs. They wanted to stay long until they saw strong bears, and since the bears demonstrated impressive strength, these bulls will look for any rally to exit. This represents supply over the market and will work to limit the rally and increase the chances of another leg down. The rally will likely have many bear bars and tails, both of which indicate that the bulls are weak. A sell-off down from this rally would create the first lower high in a potential new bear trend. In any case, the odds are high that there will be a second leg down since both the bulls and the bears expect it and will be trading accordingly.

There will still be bulls who bought much lower and want to give the bull trend every possible chance to resume. Traders know that most reversal attempts fail, and many who rode the trend up will not exit their longs until after the bears have demonstrated the ability to push the market down hard. Many longs bought puts to protect themselves in case of a severe reversal. The puts allow them to hold on to give the bull trend every possible chance to resume. They know that the puts limit their losses, no matter how far the market might fall, but once they see this impressive selling pressure, they will then look for a rally to finally exit their longs and will take profits on their puts as the market turns back up. Also, most of their puts expire within a few months, and once expired, the traders no longer have downside protection. This means that they cannot continue to hold on to their positions unless they keep buying more and more puts. If they believe that the market will likely fall further and not rally again for many months, it does not make sense to continue to pay for ongoing put protection. Instead, they will look to sell out of their positions. Their supply will limit the rally, and their selling added to the shorting by aggressive bears and the profit-taking by bulls who saw the sell-off as a buying opportunity, will create a second leg down.

These persistent bulls will each have a price level on the downside that, if reached, will make them want to exit on the next rally. As the market keeps working lower, more and more of these bulls will decide that the bull trend will not resume anytime soon and that the trend might have reversed into a bear trend. These remaining die-hard longs will wait patiently for a pullback in the bear swing to exit their longs, and their positions represent a supply that is overhanging the market. They sell below the most recent swing high because they doubt that the market will be able to get above a prior swing high and are happy to get out at any price above the most recent low. Bears will also look for a pullback from each new low to add to their shorts and place new shorts. The result is a series of lower highs and lower lows, which is the definition of a bear trend.

Typically, the initial move will break the trend line and then form a pullback that tests the end of the old trend, and traders will look to initiate countertrend (actually with-trend, in the direction of the new trend) positions after this test.

Major Trend Reversal

There are many institutions that invest for the long term and view every strong break below the bull trend line as a buying opportunity because they know that the bears will constantly try to reverse the trend but will fail 80 percent of the time. They will buy even if the bear spike is huge and strong, and goes far below the trend line and the moving average. They hope that their buying will provide the leadership that other traders need to see before they will also buy. At a minimum, they expect the rally to test the breakout point below the market top. Once there, they will decide if the trend has reversed. If so, they will stop buying and instead will exit their new longs as well as all of the other longs that they bought all the way up. Most of their position was profitable because they bought it long ago, far below their last entry. However, since they are buying as the trend continues up, they bought some of their position at the top of the bull and will take a loss when they exit. Once these long-term investing institutions believe that the market is going lower, the trend will reverse, because they were the traders who previously bought every sharp sell-off, and now there is no one left to buy strong bear spikes. They will wait until they believe that the bear trend has reached a long-term value area, which will always be at a long-term support area, like a monthly trend line. Once there, they will buy aggressively again, and they will buy every further attempt by the bears to extend the bear trend. At some point, other institutions will see the support forming and they will also buy. There will soon be a strong bull spike, a pullback that tests the bear low, and then a reversal into a new bull trend.

Every reversal pattern is some kind of trading range and therefore has two-sided trading until it is clear that the countertrend traders have gained control. The term major trend reversal means different things to different traders, and no one can say with certainty that the trend has reversed until the move has gone on for at least enough bars for the always-in position to change direction in the eyes of most traders. However, that alone is not enough for a reversal to be labeled "major." The always-in position changes with every tradable swing on the 5-minute chart for many traders, which means that it changes many times a day on most days, even though the dominant trend usually remains the same. A major trend reversal means that there are two trends on the chart in front of you, with a reversal in between them where either a bull trend has reversed into a bear trend or a bear trend has reversed into a bull trend. This type of reversal is different from the many up and down reversals on the chart that usually move far enough for a trade, but not far enough to change the direction of the major trend. Also, those minor reversals happen whether or not there is an obvious trend on the screen.

The earliest signals for most major trend reversals have a low probability of success but offer the largest reward, often many times greater than the risk. The market is often mostly sideways at the outset, with many pullbacks, but if the trend is actually reversing, the new trend will soon be obvious. Many traders prefer to wait to enter until the trend is clear. These traders prefer to only take trades with at least a 60 percent chance of success and are willing to make less (they are entering after the move has already begun) on the trade for the increased chance of success. Since both approaches have positive trader's equations when done properly, both are reasonable. Here's what a major trend reversal looks like:

Four things are needed for a major trend reversal:

1. A trend on the chart in front of you.
2. A countertrend move (a reversal) that is strong

enough to break the trend line and usually the moving average.
3. A test of the trend's extreme, and then a second reversal (a higher high, a double top, or a lower high at the top of a bull trend, or a lower low, a double bottom, or a higher low at the bottom of a bear trend).
4. The second reversal going far enough for there to be a consensus that the trend has reversed.

First, there has to be a trend on the screen in front of you, and then a countertrend move that is strong enough to break the major trend's trend line, and preferably convincingly beyond the moving average. Next, the trend has to resume and test the old trend's extreme, and then the market has to reverse again. For example, after there is a strong move down below the bull trend line in a bull trend, traders will watch the next rally. If the market turns down again in the area of the old high (from a lower high, double top, or higher high), the test was successful and traders will begin to suspect that the trend is reversing.

FINALLY, the move down has to be strong enough for traders to believe that the market is in a bear trend. If the move down is in the form of a strong bear spike composed of many consecutive large bear trend bars, everyone will see the market as now being in a bear trend. However, the market will instead often be in a broad bear channel for 50 or more bars, without enough clarity to convince traders that the trend has truly reversed to down. They may wonder if it instead has evolved into a large trading range, which will often be the case. In the absence of a very strong bear spike, there will not be strong agreement that the trend has reversed until after dozens of bars and a series of lower highs and lows. At this point, the market can be far below the old bull high and there might not be much more left to the bear trend.

It does not matter that agreement about the reversal often does not come until long after the market has actually reversed because there will be trades all the way down. If the move down is unclear and two-sided, traders will trade it like any other two-sided market and take trades in both directions. If it is a very strong bear trend, traders will almost exclusively take shorts. If there are trades all the way down, then why should a trader ever think about a major trend reversal? Because the trader's equation is excellent if a trader enters early, just as the market is turning down from its test of the old high. The reward is often many times larger than the risk, and even if the probability is only 40 to 50 percent, the result is a very favorable trader's equation. Most lead to trading ranges, but still profitable trades.

VIRTUALLY ALL MAJOR trend reversals begin with either a trend line break or a trend channel line overshoot and reversal, and all of those eventually break the trend line when there is a reversal. For example, if a bull market is ending in a head and shoulders top, the move down from the head usually breaks below the bull trend line for the entire bull trend, and always below the smaller bull trend line along the bottom of the bars that rally up to form the head. The bulls buy when the sell-off from the head reaches the area of the pullback from the left shoulder, trying to create a double bottom bull flag. Many bears, who shorted as the rally to the head moved above the left shoulder, take profits in the same area, in case the market enters a trading range or forms a double bottom bull flag. The bears see the rally that creates the right shoulder as a lower high breakout pullback short setup, and short. The trend line break is what a bear needs to see before feeling confident about taking a countertrend position (a short in a bull trend) because it signifies a break of the trend and the start of a possible major trend reversal. Also, bulls who bought at the prior high (the head), expecting another leg up, and held on to their positions watch the strength of the sell-off from the head. Once they see that it was strong enough to fall below the trend line, they will use the rally to exit their longs with a small loss. The selling by both the bulls and the bears causes the market to drop and form the lower high (the right shoulder). Once the market sells off to the neckline (a roughly horizontal line drawn across the bottom of the pattern, along with the lowest points of the sell-offs from the left shoulder, head, and finally right shoulder), both the bulls and the bears will assess the strength of the sell-off. If it is strong, the bears will no longer simply scalp out of their shorts, thinking that the market is still in a trading range. Instead, they will hold on to their shorts and even sell more, expecting a major trend reversal, especially on and after the breakout below the neckline. The bulls will see the strength of the selling and will not be willing to buy until the market stabilizes, which they expect will be at least several bars later, and possibly after a measured move down.

If, in contrast, the sell-off from the head to the neckline is weak, both the bulls and the bears will buy on the test of the neckline. The bulls will buy because they see the entire pattern as a trading range in a bull trend and therefore just a large bull flag. They are buying what they expect is the bottom of the bull flag, where there is an approximate triple bottom (the three reversals up from the neckline). Some bulls will scalp out as the market tests toward the middle or top of the trading range, and others will hold, looking for a bull breakout and a swing up. The bears will buy back their shorts and not look to sell again until they can get a better price. They hope that the bounce stays below the right shoulder, and if it does or if it forms a double top with the right shoulder, they will short again, hoping that the pattern becomes a head and shoulders top with two right shoulders, which is common. If the market breaks above the right shoulder, they will buy back their shorts and not look to sell again for many bars, concluding that the entire pattern evolved into a large bull flag and that the breakout will likely rally for at least a measured move up. The bulls will also buy the breakout above the right shoulder, knowing that the bears will cover their shorts and not look to sell again for many bars. They, like the bears, will expect an approximately measured move up and will buy more as the new bull leg progresses.

THE SAME IS true of a double top or a higher high. Whenever the market returns to the area of a prior high after having a sharp sell-off, the bulls who bought at the old high become disappointed by that sell-off and use the rally to exit their longs. This means that they become sellers (they sell out of their longs), and they won't buy again until prices get marked down considerably. With no one left to buy at the current prices and both the bulls and bears selling, the market falls.

. . .

THE SAME HAPPENS at a market bottom. Once there is a rally that is strong enough to break above the bear trend line (either the trend line for the entire bear trend or simply the one above the sell-off to the head), the bears who shorted at the bottom as the market broke below the left shoulder, expecting another leg down, will be disappointed by the rally and will expect at least another leg up after a test down. Traders will see the next leg down as a test of the strength of the bear trend. If the bear trend is strong, the market will eventually break below the old low (the head) by many bars and have another leg down. If the trend is reversing, aggressive bulls will buy around the old low, and the bears who shorted at the old low will be disappointed by the strong rally from the head, and the weaker move down to test the bear low, and will use this dip to buy back their shorts around breakeven. With both the bulls and the bears buying, and the bears unwilling to sell again around this level, the market will rally. This test can form a perfect double bottom with the old bear low, a higher low, or a lower low. It does not matter, because they are all manifestations of the same process. If it forms a higher low, some traders will see it as a right shoulder of a head and shoulders bottom and will look for a reasonable left shoulder. If they find one, they will be more confident that this is a trend reversal because they believe that many traders will recognize the pattern and begin to buy. However, whether there is a clear left shoulder is irrelevant to most traders. The important point is that there is a strong break above the bear trend line, followed by a test of the bear low, and then by a reversal up into a bull swing or trend.

. . .

WHETHER A TOP COMES from a higher high, a perfect double top, or a lower high is irrelevant, because they all represent the same behavior. The market is testing the old high to see if there will be mostly buyers and a bull breakout, or mostly sellers and a bear reversal. There are two pushes up to the top: the first is the original bull high, and the second is the test of that high after the market has fallen below the bull trend line. The market does not care how perfect the double top is; regardless of their appearance, all of the tests should be thought of as variations of double tops. The same is true of market bottoms. There is a market low and then a rally that is usually strong enough to break above the bear trend line. That low is the first bottom of the double bottom. After the market breaks above the bear trend line (and therefore out of the bear channel) and sells off again to test the first bottom, when the market reverses up, this low is the second bottom of the double bottom, whether it is above, exactly at, or below the first bottom.

The relationship between traditional double tops and bottoms and their micro versions on higher time frame charts is the same as it is for all micro patterns. For example, if a trader sees a double bottom on a 5-minute chart and then looks at a higher time frame chart, the two bottoms will be just two or three bars apart, creating a micro double bottom. Similarly, if a trader looks at a micro double bottom on the 5-minute chart where the two bottoms are just two or three bars apart, this bottom would be a perfect trend reversal on a small-enough time frame chart, where the rally after the first bottom broke above the bear trend line, and the second bottom is the test. In fact, most tradable reversals on every chart, even small scalps, begin with a micro double bottom or top, and most traders will not place the reversal trade unless one is present. A micro double top is a failed breakout in a bull trend, and therefore either a failed high 1, high 2, or triangle buy signal, and a failed double bottom is a failed low 1, low 2, or a triangle sell signal. This means that these reversals are small final flag reversals. In fact, a final flag is a variation of a double top or bottom. For example, if there is a two-legged rally on a trading range day and the market then forms an ii pattern, traders will be alert to a possible final flag breakout and reversal down.

THE SPIKE that formed just before the ii patterns is the first push-up, and the small bull breakout is the second. Since that is two pushes up, even though the highs are not at the same level, it is just a variation of a double top.

Traders anticipating a reversal down will short at and above the high of the signal bar for the breakout of what they anticipate will be the final bull flag. When it is a micro pattern, their limit orders to short will be at and just above the high of the signal bar. When it is a larger pattern, it will be a micro pattern on a higher time frame chart, and some traders will have their limit orders at and above that higher time frame signal bar. Other traders, and probably many institutions, will scale into shorts as the market moves out of what they believe will be the final bull flag. They do the opposite at market bottoms with a double bottom or micro double bottom that they expect will become the final flag of the bear leg and lead to a reversal up.

Remember, all trends are in channels, and until there is a strong breakout of the channel, the best bet is against any attempt to break out beyond the trend line. Until there is a strong break beyond the trend line, most traders will view any countertrend trade as only a scalp. In the absence of a trend line break, there is still a strong trend in effect and traders should make sure that they take every with-trend entry and do not worry about missing an occasional countertrend scalp. The best odds and the most money are with the with-trend trades. True V bottoms and tops in the absence of trend channel line overshoots and reversals are so rare that they are not worth considering. Traders should focus on common patterns, and if they miss an occasional rare event, there will always be a pullback where they can start trading with the new trend.

The trend line break does not reverse the trend. It is simply the first significant sign that countertrend traders are getting strong enough that you should soon begin to trade in their direction. However, you first should continue to trade with the trend because after the break of the trend line there will be a test of the old trend extreme. The test can slightly overshoot or undershoot the old extreme. You should take a countertrend trade only if a reversal setup develops during this test. If it does, the countertrend move should form at least two legs, and it might even result in a new, opposite trend.

A MOVE above a prior high in a bull trend will generally lead to one of three outcomes: more buying, profit-taking, or shorting. When the trend is strong, strong bulls will press their longs by buying the breakout above the old high and there will be a measured move up of some kind. If the market goes up far enough above the breakout to enable a trader to make at least a profitable scalp before there is a pullback, then assume that there was mostly new buying at the high. If it goes sideways, assume that there was profit-taking and that the bulls are looking to buy again a little lower. If the market reverses down hard, assume that the strong bears dominated at the new high and that the market will likely trade down for at least a couple of legs and at least 10 bars.

Some traders like to enter on the earliest sign that a trend is reversing, such as when it is breaking out of the channel. However, this is a low-probability style of trading. Yes, the large reward can offset the risk and low probability of success, but most traders end up cherry-picking and invariably talking themselves out of the best cherries. As with all breakouts, it is usually better to wait to see how strong the breakout is. If it is strong, then look to enter on the pullback. This concept applies to reversals from all trends, even small trends, like pullbacks in larger trends, microchannels, channels after spikes, and trends that are in broad channels. If the countertrend breakout is weak, look to enter in the direction of the trend as the reversal attempt fails.

IN THE ABSENCE of some rare, dramatic news event, traders don't suddenly switch from extremely bullish to extremely bearish. There is a gradual transition. A trader becomes less bullish, then neutral, and then bearish. Once enough traders make this transition, the market reverses into a deeper correction or into a bear trend. Every firm has its own measure of excess, and at some point, enough firms decide that the trend has gone too far. They believe that there is little risk of missing a great move up if they stop buying above the old high, and they will buy only on pullbacks. If the market hesitates above the old high, the market is becoming two-sided, and the strong bulls are using the new high to take profits.

Profit-taking means that traders are still bullish and are looking to buy a pull-back. Most new highs are followed by profit-taking. Every new high is a potential top, but most reversal attempts fail and become the beginning of bull flags, only to be followed by another new high. If a rally to test the high has several small pullbacks within the leg up, with lots of overlapping bars, several bear bodies, and big tails on the tops of the bars, and most of the bull trend bars are weak, then the market is becoming increasingly two-sided. The bulls are taking profits at the tops of the bars and buying only at the bottoms of the bars, and the bears are beginning to short at the tops of the bars. Similarly, the bulls are taking profits as the market approaches the top of the bull trend and the bears are shorting more. If the market goes above the bull high, it is likely that the profit-taking and shorting will be even stronger, and a trading range or reversal will form.

Most traders do not like to reverse, so if they are anticipating a reversal signal, they prefer to exit their longs and then wait for that signal. The loss of these bulls on the final leg up in the trend contributes to the weakness of the rally to the final high. If there is a strong reversal down after the market breaks above the prior high, the strong bears are taking control of the market, at least for the near term.

How To Trade Reversal

When traders enter a reversal trade, they are expecting the pullback from the trend to be large enough for a swing trade, or even a trend in the opposite direction. The entry, protective stops, and profit-taking are then the same as for any other swing or trend trade. Since traders are expecting a large move, the probability of success is often 50 percent or less. In general, when risk is held constant, a larger potential reward usually means a smaller probability of success. This is because the edge in trading is always small, and if there was a high probability of success, traders would neutralize it quickly and it would disappear within a few bars, resulting in only a small profit. However, since a trend reversal trade may have a reward that is several times larger than the risk, it can have a profitable trader's equation.

Trading a reversal is much more difficult than it appears when a trader looks at a chart at the end of the day. Once there has been a strong break of the trend line and then a reversal on the test of the trend's extreme, a trader needs a strong signal bar. However, it usually comes in a very emotional market at a time when beginning traders are still thinking that the old trend is in effect. They also probably lost on several earlier countertrend trades in the day and don't want to lose any more money. Their denial causes them to miss the early entry. They then wait to evaluate the strength of the follow-through. It is usually in the form of a large, fast spike made of several strong trend bars, forcing the traders to quickly decide whether to risk much more than they usually do. They often end up choosing to wait for a pullback. Even if they reduce their position size so that the dollar risk is the same as with any other trade, the thought of risking two or three times as many ticks frighten them. Entering on a pullback is difficult because every pullback begins with a minor reversal, and they are afraid that the pullback might be the resumption of the prior trend. They end up waiting until the day is almost over, and then finally decide that the new trend is clear, but now there is no more time left to place a trade. Trends do everything that they can to keep traders out, which is the only way they can keep traders chasing the market all day. When a setup is easy and clear, the move is usually a small, fast scalp. If the move is going to go a long way, it has to be unclear and difficult to take, to keep traders on the sidelines and force them to chase the trend.

Now let's check out signs of strength in a reversal.

Signs Of Strength In Reversal

Strong reversals have essentially the same characteristics of any strong move, like a strong breakout or a strong trend. Here are a number of characteristics that are common in strong bull reversals:

- There is a strong bull reversal bar with a large bull trend body and small tails or no tails.
- The next two or three bars also have bull bodies that are at least the average size of the recent bull and bear bodies.
- The spike grows to five to 10 bars without pulling back for more than a bar or so, and it reverses many bars, swing highs, and bear flags of the prior bear trend. r One or more bars in the spike have a low

that is at or just one tick below the close of the prior bar.
- One or more bars in the spike have an open that is above the close of the prior bar.
- One or more bars in the spike have a close on the high of the bar or just one tick below its high.
- The overall context makes a reversal likely, like a higher low or lower low test of the bear low after a strong break above the bear trend line.
- The first or second bar of the breakout has a close that is above the highs of many prior bars.
- The first pullback occurs only after three or more bars.
- The first pullback lasts only one or two bars, and it follows a bar that is not a strong bear reversal bar.
- The first pullback does not hit a breakeven stop (the entry price).
- The spike goes very far and breaks several resistance levels like the moving average, prior swing highs, and trend lines, and each by many ticks.
- As the first bar of the reversal is forming, it spends most of its time near its high and the pullbacks are less than a quarter of the height of the growing bar.
- There is a sense of urgency. You feel like you have to buy but you want a pull-back, yet it never comes.
- The signal is the second attempt to reverse within the past few bars (a second signal).
- The reversal began as a reversal from an overshoot of a trend channel line from the old trend.
- It is reversing a significant swing high or low (e.g., it breaks below a strong prior swing low and reverses up).

- r The high 1 and high 2 pullbacks have strong bull reversal bars for signal bars. r It has trending "anything": closes, highs, lows, or bodies.
- The pullbacks are small and sideways. There were prior breaks of earlier bear trend lines (this isn't the first sign of bullish strength).
- The pullback to test the bear low lacks momentum, as evidenced by its having many overlapping bars with many being bull trend bars.
- The pullback that tests the bear low fails at the moving average or the old bear trend line.
- The breakout reverses many recent closes and highs. For example, when there is a bear channel and a large bull bar forms, this breakout bar has a high and close that are above the highs and closes of five or even 20 or more bars. A large number of bars reversed by the close of the bull bar is a stronger sign than a similar number of bars reversed by only its high.
- Here are a number of characteristics that are common in strong bear reversals:
- There is a strong bear reversal bar with a large bear trend body and small tails or no tails.
- The next two or three bars also have bear bodies that are at least the average size of the recent bull and bear bodies.
- The spike grows to five to 10 bars without pulling back for more than a bar or so, and it reverses many bars, swing lows, and bull flags of the prior bull trend. r One or more bars in the spike has a high that is at or just one tick above the close of the prior bar.

- One or more bars in the spike have an open that is below the close of the prior bar.
- One or more bars in the spike have a close on its low or just one tick above its low.
- The overall context makes a reversal likely, like a lower high or higher high test of the bull high after a strong break below the bull trend line.
- The first or second bar of the breakout has a close that is below the lows of many prior bars.
- The first pullback occurs only after three or more bars.
- The first pullback lasts only one or two bars and it follows a bar that is not a strong bull reversal bar.
- The first pullback does not hit a breakeven stop (the entry price).
- The spike goes very far and breaks several support levels like the moving average, prior swing lows, and trend lines, and each by many ticks.
- As the first bar of the reversal is forming, it spends most of its time near its low and the pullbacks are less than a quarter of the height of the growing bar.
- There is a sense of urgency. You feel like you have to sell, but you want a pullback, yet it never comes.
- The signal is the second attempt to reverse within the past few bars (a second signal).
- The reversal began as a reversal from an overshoot of a trend channel line from the old trend.
- It is reversing at a significant swing high or low area (e.g., breaks above a strong prior swing high and reverses down).
- The low 1 and low 2 pullbacks have strong bear reversal bars for signal bars.
- It has to trend "anything": closes, highs, lows, or

bodies.
- The pullbacks are small and sideways.
- There were prior breaks of earlier bull trend lines (this isn't the first sign of bearish strength).
- The pullback to test the bull high lacks momentum, as evidenced by it having
- many overlapping bars with many being bear trend bars.
- The pullback that tests the bull high fails at the moving average or the old bull trend line.
- The breakout reverses many recent closes and lows. For example, when there is a bull channel and a large bear bar forms, this breakout bar has a low and close that is below the lows and closes of five or even 20 or more bars. A large number of bars reversed by the close of the bear bar is a stronger sign than a similar number of bars reversed by its low.

SOME REVERSALS RESULT in trend reversals and others simply in small countertrend swings. Carefully analyzing the price action before and after the reversal helps traders gauge how much if any of their position they should swing and how big a move to anticipate. When there is a strong trend, traders should not be taking countertrend trades until there has been a trend line break or at least a climactic reversal from a trend channel line overshoot. In a trading range market, however, traders can trade reversals in both directions.

There are many characteristics of strong reversals, and the more that are present, the more likely a countertrend trade will be profitable and the more aggressive traders should be in their decision about how much of their position they should swing. The stronger the prior trend line break in a trend reversal, the more likely the reversal will gain more points and last longer, and have two or more legs. The strongest trend line breaks have strong momentum and surge well past the moving average and usually beyond swing points in the prior trend.

The stronger the trend, the more likely it will need a strong reversal for a trader to make a profit from a countertrend trade. For example, if traders are looking to short a very strong bull trend, they will want to see as many signs of a strong reversal as possible. In contrast, if the bull trend has been very two-sided, they will be comfortable shorting a weaker reversal setup. If instead, the market is simply rallying to the top of a trading range, they may not even need a reversal bar when they are shorting. Finally, if the market is in a wedge bull flag and they are looking for it to reverse back up into the bull trend, they might even be willing to buy above a bear trend bar.

Incidentally, if the market is a zero-sum game, how can it have 95 percent of the participants be profitable institutions? This is because it is not really a zero-sum game. Our economy grows and therefore creates wealth. The total value of the market is greater than it was 10 years ago and far greater than 100 years ago. The firms all compete to get as much of that new wealth as possible, and there is enough to make almost all firms profitable in most years. In years when the economy contracts, most firms lose money, but during expansions, they make more than what they lose during the down years.

5
STOP-LOSS ORDERS

Understanding the Basics

A stop-loss order is an order that automatically closes a losing position once the price hits the pre-specified level. Traders are using stop-loss strategies to limit their losses and consequently protect their trading account, in case the market moves against their positions. The following strategy can also protect from potential losses if they can not access their trading accounts due to losing connection to the internet, personal problems, or for any other reason. Therefore, stop losses can play an important role in your trading strategy and in my opinion is an absolute must for novice traders to prevent large and uncontrollable losses in volatile trades. If you're not using stop-losses, it's only a matter of time when a large losing position will get out of control and wipe out most of your trading profits, eventually even your entire account!

Stop-Loss Placement Methods

Common methods include the percentage method. So if you set the stop-loss order at 10% below the price at which you purchased the security, your loss will be limited to 10%. For example, if you buy Company X's stock for $50 per share, you can enter a stop-loss order for $45. This will keep your loss to 10%. Hence if Company X's stock drops below $45, your shares will be sold at the current price.

There's also the support method which involves hard stops at a set price. This method may be a little harder to practice. You'll need to figure out the most recent support level of the stock and place your stop-loss order just below that level.

The other method is the moving average method. By using this way, stop-losses are placed just below a longer-term moving average price rather than shorter-term prices.

Swing traders often employ a multiple-day high/low method, in which stops are placed at the low price of a pre-determined day's trading. For example, lows may consistently be replaced at the two-day low. More patient traders may use indicator stops based on larger trend analysis. Indicator stops are often coupled with other technical indicators such as the Relative Strength Index (RSI) that will be discussed more in detail in a second book "Technical Analysis for the Trading Sharks: Beware Of These Stock Market Warning Signs"

Theoretical analysis of the Bear Markets

On October 7, 1998, the dollar-yen exchange rate fell 11 percent. On March 7, 2002, the rate dropped over 3 percent.

These moves, which dwarf the 0.7 percent standard deviation of daily returns in dollar-yen since 1990, are symptomatic of a broader phenomenon: the well-known "fat tails" of exchange rate returns. Since 1990, dollar-yen returns above four standard deviations have occurred 85 times more frequently than predicted by the normal distribution; under a normal distribution, daily returns above 3 percent would occur fewer than once every 100 years.1

Dramatic exchange rate moves are as puzzling to economists as they are disruptive to market participants. According to standard exchange rate models, the main force behind them must be news. Yet Cai et al. find that the arrival of news was of only "secondary importance" for extraordinary yen volatility throughout 1998. Likewise, Evans found out that "public news is rarely the predominant source of exchange rate movements over any horizon." Of greater importance.

Researchers have also turned to order flow to account for the stock market crash of 1987, another dramatic price move that cannot be explained by the news. Theoretical analyses have highlighted an important role for portfolio insurance and stop-loss orders, two trading schemes in which sell (buy) orders are triggered by a price decline (rise) to a pre-specified level. Because these schemes involve price contingent, positive feedback trading, they can contribute to market discontinuities that are, crashes under imperfect information. In the most commonly cited scenario, a price decline from any source triggers portfolio insurance sales, which further depress prices, which triggers additional portfolio insurance sales, etc. This type of self-reinforcing price dynamic will be referred to here as a "price cascade." Since information about portfolio insurance and stop-loss orders is not public, rational trading by uninformed agents could intensify such a price cascade.

WE'LL BE USING this theoretical analysis of the 1987 stock market crash to help explain the high frequency of large exchange rate moves. In what is, to the author's knowledge, the first empirical attempt to examine the effects of price-contingent positive-feedback trading, the chapter asks, Do stop-loss orders contribute to price cascades in currency markets? The evidence presented here suggests that the answer is Yes. Here's what a stop-loss order looks like:

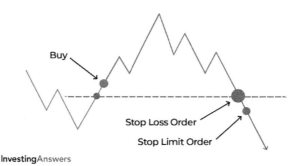

This idea is hardly new. Among market participants, it is common knowledge that stop-loss orders contribute to price cascades. With regard to the March 7, 2002 drop-in dollar-yen, for example, Deutsche Bank noted the following: "Without any news to trigger the move, Japanese accounts aggressively sold USD/JPY, which in turn triggered successive waves of stop-loss orders. The first wave of stop-loss selling occurred on the break of •130.50 and then again on the break of •130. Once below •129.80, USD/JPY fell within seconds to •129.40 . . .". Likewise, the currency market newsletter to which this author subscribes reported that "stops were triggered," or some equivalent, on at least 16 of the approximately 190 trading days from December 2000 through August 2001, or at least once every two weeks. Market lore suggests that participants sometimes intentionally trigger a series of stop-loss orders, and the activity has:

- The normal distribution used for comparison here has the same mean and standard deviation as actual returns.
- Positive-feedback trading involves sales (purchases) following price declines (rises).
- Since currency commentators are not active market traders and their knowledge of the existence and execution of stop-loss orders is at best second-hand, it is possible that large stop-loss orders were triggered more frequently than this suggests.

This phenomenon exists in currency markets, where stop-loss orders are commonplace. To identify when such orders are executed, I turn to evidence that stop-loss orders cluster in predictable ways: stop-loss sell orders cluster just below round numbers; stop-loss buy orders cluster just above round numbers. The empirical analysis, therefore, focuses on high-frequency exchange rate behavior near round numbers. The tests rely on minute-by-minute exchange rate quotes for dollar-mark, dollar-yen, and dollar-U.K. pound during New York trading hours from January 1996 through April 1998. The statistical methodology is a variant of the bootstrap.

The analysis first shows that exchange rates tend to move rapidly after reaching levels where stop-loss orders cluster. This indicates that a trend can be prolonged by the execution of some stop-loss orders triggered by that trend, consistent with the chapter's main hypothesis. However, this result need not demonstrate that stop-loss orders are sometimes executed in "waves," as described by Deutsche Bank. That is, it need not indicate that the execution of stop-loss orders at one level sometimes propels rates to new levels, thereby triggering more stop-loss orders.

To evaluate whether stop-loss orders are actually triggered in waves, the chapter undertakes two tests in which exchange rate behavior after reaching stop-loss orders is compared with behavior after reaching other orders, called "take-profits." Take-profit orders instruct dealers to buy (sell) a certain amount of currency if the rate falls (rises) to a particular level. Here's what a Take-profit order looks like:

Take-profit orders differ from stop-loss orders in that they generate negative feedback trading, as a result of which take-profit orders should not contribute to price cascades and would never be triggered in waves. Furthermore, take-profit orders cluster on, rather than near, round numbers. The two tests both exploit the observation that, if stop-loss orders are sometimes triggered in waves, the response to stop-loss orders should be larger, and should last longer, than the response to take-profit orders. Results support these implications.

This chapter evaluates the average response of exchange rates to take-profit orders, per se.

IF STOP-LOSS trading in currency markets contributes to price cascades, then it also contributes to the high frequency of large moves relative to that predicted by the normal distribution, a property known familiarly as "fat tails." Fat tails, in turn, contribute to "excess kurtosis," or kurtosis higher than the value of three associated with the normal distribution.6 Existing research on excess kurtosis in currency markets has primarily focused on its statistical origins. In addressing instead, the economic origins of excess kurtosis, this chapter joins Amihud and Mendelson, which shows that the distribution of daily NYSE returns varies with the trading process. It also joins, which shows that, for a given trading process, kurtosis is positively related to agent heterogeneity.

6

THE BEST TRADES: PUTTING IT ALL TOGETHER

The market is linear—it can only go up or down. When you plot it on a conventional chart with time on the horizontal axis, you add a second dimension, but the market itself is the only price, which means that it has only one dimension. You can make bull and bear bodies have different colors, incorporate volume into the widths of the bodies, or add all kinds of indicators, increasing the number of dimensions, but the market itself is one-dimensional. The recurring theme of these books is that the market is basically simple. It moves up or down because it is constantly searching for the best price, which changes constantly because of unending changes in countless fundamentals. The fundamentals are anything that traders feel is important and include data on every stock, the overall market, politics, natural and manmade events from earthquakes to wars, and international factors. This results in the market always trying to break out from a trading range (its current area of agreement on the value of the market) into a trend, as it searches for the appropriate instantaneous value for the market. If the breakout is to the upside, the bulls are momentarily successfully asserting their opinion that the market is too cheap. If there is instead a downside breakout, then the bears at least briefly are winning their argument that the market is too expensive. Every breakout attempt is met by traders holding the opposite belief, and they will try to make the breakout fail and the market reverse. This is true on every time frame and on every bar and series of bars. The trading range can be a single bar or a hundred bars, and the breakout can last one bar or many bars. The key to trading is developing the ability to assess whether the bulls or bears are stronger. When a trader believes that the odds favor one side over the other, he has an edge. The "odds" refers to the trader's equation. An edge (positive trader's equation) exists if the probability of trade reaching his profit target before hitting his protective stop is greater than the probability of the market hitting his stop before reaching his target.

H<small>AVING</small> an edge gives him an opportunity to make money by placing a trade. Every type of market does something to make trading difficult. The market is filled with very smart people who are trying as hard to take money from your account as you are trying to take money from theirs, so nothing is ever easy. This even includes making profits in a strong trend. When the market is trending strongly with large trend bars, the risk is great because the protective stop often belongs beyond the start of the spike. Also, the spike grows quickly, and many traders are so shocked by the size and speed of the breakout that they are unable to quickly reduce their position size and increase their stop size, and instead watch the trend move rapidly as they hope for a pullback. Swing traders are often uncomfortable entering on the spike because they prefer trades where the reward is two or more times the size of the risk. They are willing to miss a high-probability trade where the reward is only equal to the size of the risk.

Once the trend enters its channel phase, it always looks like it is reversing. For example, in a bull trend, there will be many reversal attempts, but almost all quickly evolve into bull flags. Most bull channels will have weak buy signal bars and the signals will force those bulls who prefer stop entries to buy at the top of the weak channel. This is a low-probability long trade, even though the market is continuing up. Swing traders who are comfortable taking low-probability buy setups near the top of weak bull channels love this kind of price action because they can make many times what they are risking and this more than makes up for the relatively low probability of success.

HOWEVER, it is difficult for most traders to buy low-probability setups near the top of a weak bull channel. Traders who only want to take high-probability trades often sit back and watch the trend grind higher for many bars, because there may not be a high-probability entry for 20 or more bars. The result is that they see the market going up and want to be long, but miss the entire trend. They only want a high-probability trade, like a high 2 pullback to the moving average. If they do not get an acceptable pullback, they will continue to wait and miss the trend. This is acceptable because traders should always stay in their comfort zone. If they are only comfortable taking high-probability stop entries, then they are correct in waiting. The channel will not last forever, and they will soon find acceptable setups.

Experienced traders buy on limit orders around and below the lows of prior bars, and they will sometimes take some short scalps during the bull channel. Both can be high-probability trades, including the shorts if there is a strong bear reversal bar at a resistance level, and some reason to think that a pullback is imminent.

Once the channel phase ends, the market enters a trading range, where there are many strong bull spikes that race to the top and strong bear spikes that race to the bottom. Traders often focus on the strong spike and assume that the breakout will succeed. They end up buying high and selling low, which is the exact opposite of what profitable traders do. Also, the reversals down from the top and up from the bottom usually have weak signal bars, and traders find it hard to take the entries that they have to take if they expect to make money in a trading range. Within a trading range, the probability for most trades hovers around 50 percent, and only occasionally gets to around 60 percent. This means that there are few high-probability setups. Also, lots of low-probability events happen, like reversals that don't look good but still lead to big swings and no follow-through after strong spikes.

All of this makes it sound impossible to make money as a trader, but if you go back to each relevant section, you will remember that there are profitable ways to trade the market, no matter how it is behaving. Your edge is always going to be small, but if you are a careful, unemotional, and objective reader of the chart in front of you, and only look to take the best trades, you are in a position to make a living as a trader.

. . .

THERE ARE traders trading for every reason and on all time frames at every second on every chart. What generalities can be made about how discretionary traders, whether institutional or individual, will trade a bull trend? A bull trend begins with a breakout, which is a spike up and can contain one or many bull trend bars. If the breakout fails, the market will fall back into the trading range, and traders will fade the breakout (it will be a final flag reversal) and continue to trade the trading range. When a breakout is strong and successful, most discretionary traders will buy with a sense of urgency. They will buy at the market, on small pullbacks, at the close of the bar, and above each prior bar. Once the market transitions into a channel, they will buy below the low of the prior bar, like below low 1 and low 2 signal bars, expecting reversal attempts to fail (in a trend, most reversal attempts fail), and above the high of the prior bar, like above high 1, high 2, and triangle buy setups. They will then buy pullbacks from the breakouts of these small bull flags. They will even buy the first breakout of a bear microchannel in a strong bull trend, knowing that there might not be a breakout pullback setup until after the market has rallied many bars. Early on, when the trend is strong, they will buy on new breakouts above prior swing highs, but as the two-sided trading (selling pressure) increases, as seen by more and larger bear trend bars and more bars with tails on their top, traders will begin to sell above prior swing highs. Most will be selling to take profits on their longs, but as the slope of the channel becomes flatter and the pullbacks become deeper, more traders will start to short above swing highs, looking for scalps. When the two-sided trading increases to the point that the bears are about as strong as the bulls, traders will see the market as having entered a trading range. This means that they are much less certain that the trend will resume on each rally attempt (they no longer are looking for pullbacks in a strong bull trend, where the breakout usually quickly tests the old high). They will buy low, sell high, and most will scalp. They will look for high 1 and high 2 buy setups near the top of the range and will short above the signal bars, instead of buying up there. At first, they will only look for scalps, like pullbacks to the moving average, the bottom of the trading range, or the bottom of the bull channel. Once they see increasing selling pressure, they will begin to swing some and eventually all of their shorts, and will only look to buy deep pullbacks, lasting 10 or more bars and having two or more legs. After there have been one or more pullbacks where the selling was strong enough to break below the trend line and below the moving average, some bears will look to short the test of the bull trend high, expecting a major trend reversal. They will short a reversal setup at a lower high, a double top, or a higher high, even though they realize that the chance of a swing down might be 40 percent or less. As long as the reward is much larger than the risk, they have a positive trader's equation, even though the chance of success is relatively low. Bulls will buy reasonable setups at the bottom of the trading range, like on larger high 2 buy setups, wedge bull flags, higher time frame trend lines, and measured move targets. Traders realize that a trading range is simply a pullback on a higher time frame chart. When the spike and channel are steep on a 5-minute chart, they together form a simple spike on a higher time frame chart, like a 15 or 60-minute chart. The trading range on the 5-minute chart is usually just a pullback on a 15 or 60-minute chart. When bulls buy near the bottom of a 5-minute trading range, many will hold for a swing up, a breakout to a new high, and a measured move up, even though the probability may be less than 50 percent. This relatively low-probability swing long has a positive trader's equation because the reward is much larger than the risk.

WHILE IN THE trading range phase, signals are often unclear, and there is a sense of uncertainty. Most of the signals will be micro double bottoms and tops, and small final flag reversals. This is lower probability trading, and traders have to be careful and quick to take profits (scalp). They must force themselves to buy low and sell high, not buy strong bull spikes near the top of the range and short strong bear spikes near the bottom. Invariably, the spikes look strong, but don't overlook all of the bars before them—in a trading range, most breakout attempts fail. Once the market has entered a trading range, if a leg is in a strong microchannel, lasting four or more bars, don't enter on the breakout. Wait to see if the breakout is strong. If so, enter on the pullback from the breakout. If there is a bear micro channel down to the bottom of the range, wait for the bull breakout and look to buy the pullback, whether it forms a higher low, a micro double bottom, or a lower low. If there is a bull micro channel up to the top of the range, wait to sell a lower high, micro double top, or higher high pullback. As with all trades, always make sure that there is an appropriate signal bar.

If the market enters a tight trading range, wait for the breakout, because tight trading ranges trump everything, including every logical reason to take a trade. Using stop entries in a tight trading range is a losing strategy, but the setups always look worthwhile. Instead, patiently wait for the breakout and then decide if it is likely to succeed or fail.

. . .

If there is a successful breakout of the top of the entire trading range, the process starts all over again. Traders will see the breakout as a spike and they will look for at least a measured move up. If there is an upside breakout, but it fails and the market reverses, traders will view the trading range as the final flag in the bull trend. If there is then a breakout below the trading range, traders will evaluate the strength of the breakout, and if it is strong, they will repeat the entire process in the opposite direction. The downside breakout from the trading range can occur without first having a failed upside breakout. Instead of a final flag reversal, the trading range can be some other kind of reversal setup, like a double top, a triple top, a head and shoulders top, or a triangle. All that matters is that there is a strong downside breakout, and traders will then expect pullbacks and a bear channel to follow the bear breakout, and then the market to evolve into a trading range, which can be then followed by a bull or bear breakout.

Examples Of Best Trades

• Opening reversals where the setup is strong

• Swing for a reward that is at least twice the risk: the probability of success is 50 to 60 percent.

• Scalp for a reward that is at least as large as the risk: the probability is about 60 to 70 percent.

• Strong reversals, where the reward is at least twice the risk and the probability is 50 to 60 percent

- Major trend reversal: Following a strong break of the trend line, look for a weak trend resumption to fail on a test of the trend's extreme; the reversal signal bar should be strong. After a bear trend, look to buy a higher low, double bottom, or lower low. After a bull trend, look to short a higher high, double top, or lower high.

- Strong final flag reversal after a swing up or down in a trading range or weak channel.

- Buying a third or fourth push down in a bear stairs pattern for a test of the low of the prior push down.

- Selling a third or fourth push-up in a bull stairs pattern for a test of the high of the prior push-up.

- Trading when the channel in a spike and channel day or the breakout in a trending trading range day reaches a measured move target and the move is weakening.

- Buying a high 2 pullback to the moving average in a bull trend. r Selling a low 2 pullback to the moving average in a bear trend. r Buying a wedge bull flag pullback in a bull trend.

- Selling a wedge bear flag pullback in a bear trend.

- Buying a breakout pullback after a breakout from a bull flag in a bull trend.

- Selling a breakout pullback after a breakout from a bear flag in a bear trend.

- Buying a high 1 pullback in a strong bull spike in a bull trend, but not after a strong buy climax.

- Selling a low 1 pullback in a strong bear spike in a bear trend, but not after a strong sell climax.

- Shorting at the top of a trading range, especially if it is a second entry.

- Buying at the bottom of a trading range, especially if it is a second entry.

- Entering using limit orders requires more experience reading charts because the traders are entering a market that is going in the opposite direction to their trade. Traders should only use limit orders to trade in the direction of the trend. For example, if a trader is thinking about using a limit order to buy at the low of the prior bar, he should only do so if the market is always-in long, or he thinks that it is likely to immediately switch to always-in long. He should never buy with the intention of scalping the long and then shorting once the low 2 sell setup forms if he believes that the market is still always-in short and is likely to have only one smaller push up. The probability of success is simply too low when using limit orders to trade countertrend. The low probability results in a losing trader's equation and you will lose money unless you are an exceptionally profitable and experienced scalper. Surprises in trends are usually in the direction of the trend, so when you think that the low 1 in a bear trend is weak and that the market should have one more push-up, the odds are too great that it will not. However, experienced traders can reliably use limit or market orders with these potential best trade setups:

- Buying a bull spike in a strong bull breakout at the market or on a limit order at or below the low of the prior bar (entering in spikes requires a wider stop and the spike happens quickly; this combination is difficult for many traders).

- Selling a bear spike in a strong bear breakout at the market or on a limit order at or above the high of the prior bar (entering in spikes requires a wider stop and the spike happens quickly; this combination is difficult for many traders).

- Buying at or below a low 1 or 2 weak signal bar on a limit order in a possible new bull trend after a strong reversal up or at the bottom of a trading range.

- Shorting at or above a high 1 or 2 weak signal bar on a limit order in a possible new bear trend after a strong reversal down or at the top of a trading range.

- Buying at or below the prior bar on a limit order in a quiet bull flag at the moving average.

- Shorting at or above the prior bar on a limit order in a quiet bear flag at the moving average.

- Buying below a bull bar that breaks above a bull flag, anticipating a breakout pullback.

- Selling above a bear bar that breaks below a bear flag, anticipating a breakout pullback.

- When trying for a swing in a bull trend, buying or buying more on a breakout test, which is an attempt to run breakeven stops from an earlier long entry.

- When trying for a swing in a bear trend, selling or selling more on a breakout test, which is an attempt to hit breakeven stops from an earlier short entry.

- Buying a pullback in a strong bull trend at a fixed number of ticks down equal to or slightly less than the average prior pullbacks.

- Selling a pullback in a strong bear trend at a fixed number of ticks up equal to or slightly less than the average prior pullbacks.

- When a bear trend is about to break into a bull trend and needs one more bull trend bar to confirm the always-in reversal, and the breakout does not look strong, sell the close of the bull breakout bar, expecting the follow-through bar not to confirm the always-in flip and the bear trend to resume.

- When a bull trend is about to break into a bear trend and needs one more bear trend bar to confirm the always-in reversal, and the breakout does not look strong, buy the close of the bear breakout bar, expecting the follow-through bar not to confirm the always-in flip and the bull trend to resume.

Top 10 Rules For Successful Trading

Here are some guidelines that beginners should consider following until they are consistently profitable (at that point, they can expand their repertoire):

- Take a trade only where you are going for a reward that is at least as large as your risk. When starting out, focus on trades where the reward is at least twice as large as the risk.

- Take trades only if you think they probably will work. Don't even worry about how far the move might go. You have to simply ask yourself if the setup looks good. If so, you should assume that the probability is at least 60 percent. With the potential reward at least as large as the risk, this creates a positive trader's equation.

- Enter only on stops.

- Always have a protective stop in the market, because belief and hope will not. protect against a premise that is failing.

- Have a profit-taking limit order in the market so that you will not get greedy. and watch your profit disappear as you hope for more.

- Buy only above bull bars and short below bear bars.

- Trade only a small position size. If you think that you can trade 300 shares, you should trade only 100 shares so that you are in "I don't care" mode. This will allow you to be more objective and less easily swayed by emotions.

- Look for only three to five reasonable trades a day. If in doubt, stay out.

- Look for simple strategies. If something is not clear, wait.

- The best choices for a trader starting out are trends that develop in the opening range, strong trend reversals, and pullbacks in strong trends.

How Much Do You Buy or Sell?

Many traders try as much as possible to avoid the reality of this question. This question clearly explains money management. It's quite critical to the success of a trader. Let's explain the concept better using an example:

Hypothetically, you've got a certain amount of cash, at this point, you get to ask yourself the question of "how much is best to trade?" being more practical, let's say you've $10,000, how much of this total amount would you want to trade? Will you be smart to ask yourself this question or you will just decide to trade all you've? If you decide to trade all you've, what if you lose all $10,000?

Well, making the best decisions in this kind of situation means investing only about 2 percent of your capital. 2 percent of $10,000 means investing only $200. At the point of making this decision, you might as well say to yourself "What is the deal?' I have got $10,000 why invest $200? Isn't that too small? Well, that's not the point. You can't possibly predict the trend's movement, so why not take a calculated risk? This brings us to the end of this chapter and ultimately, the end of this book.

CONCLUSION

With over six chapters discussed in this book, we have been able to cover the major tenets of trading, all the basics of trading that all rookies and veterans need to get familiar with. Ranging from technical analysis, breakouts and pullbacks, trading charts, trading signals, and ultimately, the basics of trading. About technical analysis, here is what you need to remember:

There's always evidence supporting the importance of moving averages, trading patterns, support, and chart momentum. However, there's no convincing evidence to back up the support of Gann Theory. We also learned that Technical analysis works best on current market happenings, future markets, and also stock markets.

We also go to understand that chat patterns work better on currency markets than markets concerning stocks. We also learned that nonlinear methods work the best when the technical analysis is in play. Technical analysis isn't as convincing as it used to be, you'll also get to understand why in this book.

Either as a rookie or veteran trader, it's very important for you to be able to read trading charts and also have the ability to depict markers and different movements on the chart, this book makes you understand that with sound knowledge on how to read and interpret charts, you'll be able to make better trading decisions.

Technical analysis is one of those strongholds of trading where different people have different opinions on what actually works and what doesn't seem forthcoming. In this book, we also discussed back-testing, explaining that it means looking back at past trading years studying the chart during those periods to possibly predict correctly the actions of forthcoming stock. This book pushes this agenda because it allows you to do your homework first before engaging in trading activities.

Still trying to make you get a better picture, check out major points about technical analysis from this book, that you shouldn't let go off your memory:

• Technical analysis is a smart method of evaluating assets and securities using statistics created by several trading activities, volume, and past price actions.

• The benefit of making use of a bar chart over a line graph is that it indicates the low, open, high, and close points of everyday trading activities.

• One of the best and most efficient technical analysis indicators to use is the moving average, the moving average shows the average price of assets or security's price over a long period. Common averages utilized include; 20,30,50,100 and 200.

Conclusion

- Support and resistance stages are price stages at which movement should either stop and change direction. Think of Support/Resistance as stages that act as a ceiling or a floor to future price fluctuations.

- There are literally several hundreds of distinct price patterns and technical analysis indicators in the market.

- In our humble opinion, technical analysis is a great tool, but much more efficient when related to the basics of fundamental analysis.

The trend reversal discussed in this book also thought us the following:

- Never try catching a falling knife or decide to trade the initial pullback happening after a downtrend

- Try to understand the four levels of the market so you get to know when price fluctuations get to cause a trend reversal

- The major setups related to a trend reversal. These setups include: breakouts, pullback, and ultimately resistance and support

- It's very possible to input a limit order or give time for a proposed candlestick chart pattern to define your entry

- Stop losses should only be set at points where if attained, your trading setup becomes invalid and the trade becomes pointless

- There are two major ways of exiting your trades, you either capture a swing or comfortably ride the trade trend.

Now that you have all the tools, go out there and use them. Be prepared for the best trading deals you can ever have.

If you enjoyed the book, please leave a review on Amazon.

Click here to join our Facebook group

Printed in France by Amazon
Brétigny-sur-Orge, FR